PEOPLES
of
AFRICA

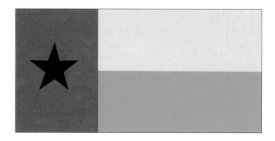

Guinea-Bissau

Ivory Coast

Kenya

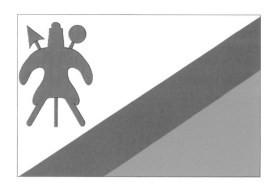

Lesotho

Liberia

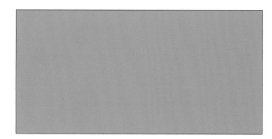

Libya

PEOPLES
of
AFRICA

Volume 5
Guinea-Bissau–Libya

MARSHALL CAVENDISH
NEW YORK • LONDON • TORONTO • SYDNEY

Marshall Cavendish Corporation
99 White Plains Road
Tarrytown, New York 10591-9001

Reference Edition 2003

Consultants:
Bryan Callahan, Department of History, Johns Hopkins University
Kevin Shillington

Pronunciation Consultant: Nancy Gratton

Contributing authors:
  Fiona Macdonald
  Elizabeth Paren
  Kevin Shillington
  Gillian Stacey
  Philip Steele

Discovery Books
  Managing Editor: Paul Humphrey
  Project Editor: Helen Dwyer
  Text Editor: Valerie J. Weber
  Design Concept: Ian Winton
  Designer: Barry Dwyer
  Cartographer: Stefan Chabluk

Marshall Cavendish
  Editorial Director: Paul Bernabeo
  Editor: Marian Armstrong

The publishers would like to thank the following for their permission to reproduce photographs:
  Robert Estall Photo Library (Carol Beckwith: cover, 246; Carol Beckwith/Angela Fisher: 241, 257, 258; David Coulson: 256; Fabby Nielsen: 259 top); Werner Forman Archive (Entwistle Gallery, London, UK: 238); gettyone Stone (Art Wolfe: 250); Hutchison Library (248; Sarah Murray: 236, 242; Trevor Page: 235; Bernard Régent: 279, 283); ICCE Photolibrary (Philip Steele: 259 bottom); Panos Pictures (Neil Cooper: 254, 260, 263, 264; Heldur Netocny: 244, 273; Caroline Penn: 277, 281; Giacomo Pirozzi: 231, 233, 234, 245, 269 bottom; Betty Press: 240, 251; Rui Vieira: 265; Lana Wong: 253); Still Pictures (Mark Edwards: 239, 243, 252; Ron Giling: 266, 269 top, 271, 272; Paul Harrison: 262); John Tough (280); Tropix Photographic Library (K. Porter: 274, 278, 282; J. Schmid: 255)

(cover) A nomadic Wodaabe mother from the Sahel in Niger carries her child on her back.

Editor's note: Many systems of dating have been used by different cultures throughout history. *Peoples of Africa* uses B.C.E. (Before Common Era) and C.E. (Common Era) instead of B.C. (Before Christ) and A.D. (Anno Domini, "In the Year of the Lord") out of respect for the diversity of the world's peoples.

Library of Congress Cataloging-in-Publication Data

Peoples of Africa.
      p. cm.
   Includes bibliographical references and index.
   Contents: v. 1. Algeria–Botswana — v. 2. Burkina-Faso–Comoros — v. 3. Congo,
Democratic Republic of–Eritrea — v. 4. Ethiopia–Guinea — v. 5. Guinea-Bissau–Libya —
v. 6. Madagascar–Mayotte — v. 7. Morocco–Nigeria — v. 8. Réunion–Somalia — v. 9.
South Africa–Tanzania — v. 10. Togo–Zimbabwe — v. 11. Index.
   ISBN 0-7614-7158-8 (set)
      1. Ethnology—Africa—Juvenile literature. 2. Africa—History—Juvenile literature. 3.
Africa—Social life and customs—Juvenile literature. I. Marshall Cavendish Corporation.

GN645 .P33 2000
305.8'0096—dc21

                                                                     99-088550

   ISBN 0-7614-7158-8 (set)
   ISBN 0-7614-7163-4 (vol. 5)

Printed in Hong Kong

06 05 04 03   6   5   4   3   2

Contents

GUINEA-BISSAU

GUINEA-BISSAU, ON THE WEST COAST OF AFRICA, is one of the smallest countries on the continent.

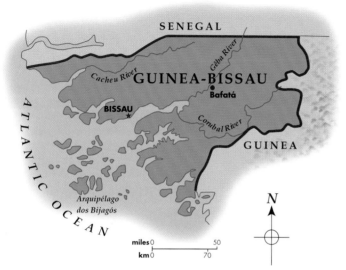

Guinea-Bissau includes the scattered Arquipélago dos Bijagós (Bijagos Archipelago), which contains sixteen fairly large islands and dozens of smaller ones.

Most of Guinea-Bissau is a low-lying, swampy, coastal plain. Traveling in this region is difficult, except by boat. The coastal plain gradually slopes upward to a plateau in the east.

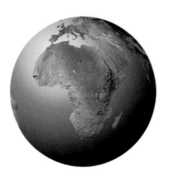

CLIMATE

Temperatures remain at the same high level year-round, but there are two main seasons. The wet season lasts from June to November; the dry season from December to May. Away from the coast, slightly less rain falls.

Average January temperature: *80°F (27°C)*

Average July temperature: *80°F (27°C)*

Average annual precipitation: *77 in. (196 cm)*

Slaves and the Portuguese

Little is known about the early history of the peoples of Guinea-Bissau (GIH-nee bih-SOW), but nine hundred years ago, Balante (buh-LAHN-tuh), Pepel (peh-PEHL), and Byago (bih-YAH-goe) people were living in the region. From around 1200 to 1400 C.E. the region was ruled by the Mali Empire (see MALI). Even before that time, the Fulani (foo-LAH-nee), who arrived from the northeast, were probably living there.

In 1466 the Portuguese were the first Europeans to land. Originally they came in search of gold, ivory, and pepper, but once Europeans began organizing huge sugar plantations in the Americas, slave trading became more profitable.

The Portuguese had rivals, especially among slave traders from Great Britain and France. All European settlements were based on the coast. Inland, the Malinke (muh-LIHN-keh) and Fulani peoples controlled the slave trade. They captured and sold as slaves mostly Pepel and Mandyako (mahn-dee-YAH-koe) peoples. Along the coast the Byago people went slave raiding in fast canoes. In return for selling slaves, African traders and

FACTS AND FIGURES

Official name: *Republica da Guiné-Bissau*

Status: *Independent state*

Capital: *Bissau*

Other town: *Bafatá*

Area: *13,948 square miles (36,125 square kilometers)*

Population: *1,200,000*

Population density: *86 per square mile (33 per square kilometer)*

Peoples: *30 percent Balante; 20 percent Fulani; 14 percent Mandyako; 13 percent Malinke; 7 percent Pepel; 3 percent Byago; also Cape Verdean, Portuguese, and Lebanese*

Official language: *Portuguese*

Currency: *Guinea peso*

National days: *Heroes' Day (January 20); Dockers' Memorial Day (September 3); Independence Day (September 24)*

Country's name: *Guinea may be derived from Djenné, the old trading center, now in Mali, or from the Ghana empire, or it may come from the berber word aguinaw, meaning "black man." Bissau is the name of the capital city and comes from bijuga, a local name for the people living in the area.*

Verde to set up peanut and oil-palm plantations along the riverbanks. Portuguese, French, and Cape Verdean trading companies ran Portuguese Guinea solely for their own profit, which meant that the African plantation workers were treated little better than slaves. Plantation owners faced fierce rebellions from the local peoples, especially the Fulani.

After a military dictatorship took control of Portugal in 1926, Portuguese Guinea was brought under strict control. Large areas of mangrove swamp and rain forest were cut down and turned into government-run plantations. Africans were forced to work wherever the government directed.

In 1956 African traders and Cape Verdean government employees secretly formed the African Party for the Independence of Guinea and Cape Verde, (in Portuguese, Partido Africano da Independência da Guiné e Cabo Verde, or

Market traders display their goods in a Bissau street. In front of the old Portuguese colonial buildings, a homemade cart passes. Few families can afford cars.

leaders received cloth, European metalwork and jewelry, and guns. The last big shiploads of slaves left the region in the 1840s.

Portugal formally took control of what was now called Portuguese Guinea in 1879. The Portuguese government encouraged Portuguese and mixed-race settlers from Cape

Time line:	Balante, Pepel, and Byago people living in the region	Region part of Mali Empire	Portuguese and other Europeans trade in slaves	Portugal takes formal control of Portuguese Guinea
	before ca. 1100 C.E.	ca. 1200–1400	1500s–1840s	1879

PAIGC). In 1959 Portuguese police killed fifty striking longshoremen demonstrating peacefully in Bissau. The PAIGC declared war against the Portuguese and sent squads of armed volunteers to fight for the country's freedom. These guerrilla soldiers received support from socialist countries worldwide.

By 1973 the PAIGC controlled half the country. The party held elections in the areas it dominated, won an overwhelming vote of support, and declared the country independent. Many countries worldwide recognized its government as legitimate, and Portugal was forced to hand over control in 1974.

At the time of independence Guinea-Bissau lay in ruins. Among the African population, there were few educated people and no doctors. Food was in short supply, as were imported and manufactured goods. The government was also seriously in debt.

The new PAIGC government introduced communist-style, state-run projects to reform society and the economy, but government policies led to inflation. People complained about inefficiency and accused the government of corruption and human rights abuses.

In 1986 the government introduced a capitalist economy and fewer state controls. Helped by large-scale overseas aid, it also planned projects to encourage trade and build roads, schools, and hospitals. In 1991 the government agreed to further reforms: free press, legal trade unions, and a multiparty system. In 1994 free elections were held; the PAIGC won but by a very narrow margin.

In June 1998 the army led a revolt against PAIGC leader João Bernardo Vieira. There was serious fighting in the capital, Bissau. The city was devastated, and many citizens fled to the rain forests nearby. A peace treaty was signed in November 1998. Although President Vieira remains in power, the political situation continues to be dangerous and very unstable.

Peoples, Languages, and Beliefs

The people of Guinea-Bissau can be divided by language and culture into five main groups: the Balante, the Fulani, the Mandyako, the Malinke, and the Pepel. There are also many smaller groups of African peoples, including the Byago on the islands.

In the city of Bissau and in ports along the coast live small communities of Portuguese and Lebanese, who work in businesses, stores, and the food and hospitality industries. Cape Verdeans make up only about one percent of the population but are among the best-educated, wealthiest, and most influential people in the country; they occupy many of the top jobs.

Recently tension has arisen between different peoples in Guinea-Bissau. The independence movement (and the PAIGC) was largely organized by Cape Verdeans, who were supported by the Balante. Leaders among the Fulani and the Malinke supported the Portuguese. Many African people also resent the Cape Verdeans' wealth and power.

War of liberation	Portugal grants independence	Capitalist economy introduced	Reforms allow free press, trade unions, and political parties	PAIGC wins first free elections	Army revolt and threat of civil war
1961–1973	**1974**	**1986**	**1991**	**1994**	**1998**

Villagers listen to the radio in a village square. Radios are a vital means of communication in remote country areas where roads and tracks are often impassable in the rainy season.

The official language of Guinea-Bissau is Portuguese, but few ordinary people understand it. They speak Crioulo (kree-OO-loe), a mixture of African and Portuguese words, together with their own local language or dialect.

Guinea-Bissau is home to many different religious faiths. Five out of every ten people follow African beliefs. These vary depending on local traditions, but most include reverence for unseen nature spirits and honor for dead ancestors. About four out of every ten people are Muslim, mostly among the Fulani and Malinke. Fewer than one in ten people are Christian.

Poverty Aplenty

Many people in Guinea-Bissau find it a struggle to make a living. Their country has few mineral resources, except for bauxite, which is inefficiently mined. The country's few factories concentrate on food processing and on making basic consumer goods.

Transportation and communication remain slow and difficult. Few roads cross the countryside, and only 15 percent of them are paved. In some towns the streets are surfaced with crushed oil-palm shells.

Most houses have one story and are laid out as clusters of single rooms erected around a central courtyard. Built of mud and straw or concrete, they have grass-thatch or sheet-iron roofs. A few colonial buildings still remain in coastal towns.

Today almost two hundred doctors live in Guinea-Bissau, but almost half of them work in the capital. Many people living in country districts have to rely on traditional healers or make their way to a clinic run by missionaries or aid workers from overseas. Parasite diseases are common, and AIDS is a growing problem. Few country areas have drains or clean drinking water supplies, so waterborne diseases such as dysentery and cholera cause sickness and death.

An education worker from UNICEF (the United Nations Children's Fund) helps parents discuss ways of making their village a healthier place for children to live.

along the coast. They also harvest coconuts, cashew nuts, and palm nuts, which are crushed to make oil used for cooking, soap, and cosmetics.

The Pepel and the Mandyako live in the countryside close to the capital on small, family-owned farms. They grow fruit and vegetables for the townspeople to eat. They cultivate rice, cassava, oranges, mangoes, and bananas in carefully fenced and drained garden plots, which are raised above the level of the surrounding marshlands.

Today there are over six hundred elementary schools. Even so, few pupils are able to continue their education beyond the age of twelve, and some are forced to drop out of school even earlier. Many parents do not have the money to buy clothes, books, pens, or paper. Many need the children to help around the house or in the fields.

A Living from the Land

Over 90 percent of the people earn their living from farming. The Balante people live along the southern coasts and rivers, where they have cleared marshy fields from the dense rain forests. They primarily live on small family farms and grow just enough food to survive. Rice is the main crop, but farmers also grow bananas, plantains, and cassava. Women often do much of the work in the fields; men go hunting in the rain forest or catch fish around the islands and

Carnival

The annual Carnival, held in February in Guinea-Bissau, is a tradition surviving from Portuguese colonial days. Originally a Christian festival, it was held to mark the beginning of Lent (a time of prayer and fasting before Easter). Today it is a joyful celebration of color, music, and dance. People wearing colorful masks parade through the streets, walking alongside brightly decorated floats.

The dancers are accompanied by music played on the kora *(KOE-rah), a cross between a harp and a guitar, and the* balafon *(BAH-lah-fawn), a huge xylophone with resonating gourds. Indigenous music in Guinea-Bissau is influenced by music from both Guinea and Senegal. Latin American music, brought from Portugal, is also very popular.*

Braided Hair and Gold Earrings

Few people in Guinea-Bissau can afford elaborate clothes. Most men wear simple Western-style pants and shirts or T-shirts, and most women wear blouses and long wraparound skirts made from brightly colored cloth. Out on the Bijagos Archipelago, away from the mainland, some women still wear traditional short skirts woven from palm fiber and no tops. Away from the coast the Fulani women of the inland region are famous for their brilliantly colored clothes, fancy braided hairstyles, and large, elaborate gold earrings. Sometimes their faces are tattooed as well.

The Fulani people live away from the coast. There, the climate is slightly drier and the land less waterlogged, so they are able to keep cattle and grow corn and peanuts. A few Fulani families own most of the wealth and employ poorer families as workers. Many Fulani also live in Bissau, the capital city, where they are active in trade and politics, and in several nearby countries (see SENEGAL and GUINEA). Like the Fulani, the Malinke also live inland, working as farmers and cattle herders.

On the islands, the Byago people live by fishing and by growing oil palms, coconuts, and cashews. Byago women have considerable economic power. They own the houses, each family's most valuable possession. This gives women the independence to choose the male partners they prefer rather than having marriages arranged for them by their families as in other ethnic groups in Guinea-Bissau and neighboring countries. Byago marriages are not expected to be lifelong as they are in many other cultures. A woman may have several partners during her lifetime, one after the other. Her children take her name and inherit property from her.

Rice is Guinea-Bissau's staple food, along with fruit (bananas, oranges, and mangoes are plentiful) and cashew nuts. Poor families subsist on rice and vegetables. Wealthier families can afford the added luxury of "sauce," a liquid stew made from palm oil, vegetables, peanuts, or, if possible, meat and fish. All kinds of meat are cooked and eaten, whatever hunters can catch in the rain forest or mangrove swamps. Cattle from the inland regions provide beef. Pigs are also kept in non-Muslim areas.

The fruit of the cashew tree is pounded to extract the juice, which will be made into powerful rum. Other popular drinks include lime juice and locally brewed beer.

IVORY COAST

IVORY COAST LIES ON THE SOUTHERN COAST OF WESTERN AFRICA.

Along the coast the land is low lying and marshy. Sandbars shelter wide, shallow lagoons from the strong waves and currents of the Atlantic Ocean.

About 30 miles (50 kilometers) inland from the coast begin the rain forests that stretch northward for around 190 miles (300 kilometers). As the climate becomes drier, savanna grasslands dotted with trees replace these rain forests. The far north of the country is a dusty plateau, where rough grass and thornbushes grow. The country's only mountains are in the far west.

CLIMATE

The coast is hot and humid all year, with very heavy rainfall from April to July and in October and November. The central forests and savannas are drier; their rainy season lasts from May to November. The northern plateau is slightly cooler than the central area, with less rainfall, but it can be scorched by hot, dry winds from the Sahara Desert between December and March.

Average January temperature: *80°F (27°C)*
Average July temperature: *77°F (25°C)*
Average annual precipitation:
   in the south: *99 in. (251 cm)*
   in the north: *40 in. (102 cm)*

Modern high-rise buildings line the highway running along the shores of the lagoon at Abidjan. Abidjan, Ivory Coast's largest city, is home to more than two million people.

A Land of Many Kingdoms

The first written records mentioning Ivory Coast were made by traders from northern Africa. From around 100 C.E. onward, they made long journeys across the Sahara Desert to buy slaves and gold. They met traders from the northern part of Ivory Coast at towns in present-day Mali. The dense belt of rain forest that stretched right across the country made contact between peoples of the northern region of Ivory Coast and peoples farther south difficult.

By about 700 C.E. Mandingo (mahn-DIHN-goe) peoples from the western African savanna region ruled powerful states, including Mali, which flourished from around 1200 to 1500 (see MALI and MAURITANIA). Beginning around 1400, groups of Mandingo peoples moved from the Mali Empire to settle in northern Ivory Coast.

During the early 1600s a number of peoples arrived in Ivory Coast. Kong was an Islamic kingdom in the north-central region, where the Senufo (seh-NOO-foe) people settled after 1600. It grew rich through farming and trade. At around the same time, the Kru (KROO) people, from present-day Liberia, arrived in south-western Ivory Coast. They lived by fishing and also found work as sailors on European ships. The kingdom of Jaman was also founded around 1600 by the Abron (ah-BROHN), a group of Akan-speaking people who left Ghana to escape that area's fast-growing Ashanti power (see GHANA). They settled close to the city of Bondoukou (bwan-doo-KOO), in the eastern central

region. Bondoukou became a great center of Muslim learning and trade.

From about 1750 onward three other Akan-speaking peoples created separate states of their own in Ivory Coast. All were in the eastern central region, and all were led by strong, independent rulers. The Baule (BAU-lae) settled in the lands around the city of Sakassou; traditional histories record that they were led from present-day Ghana by their queen, Aura Poku. The Indenie and the Sanwi (together sometimes called the Agni) settled nearby. From

FACTS AND FIGURES

Official name: *République de Côte d'Ivoire*

Status: *Independent state*

Capital: *Yamoussoukro*

Major towns: *Abidjan, Bouaké, Daloa*

Area: *124,503 square miles (322,463 square kilometers)*

Population: *15,800,000*

Population density: *127 per square mile (49 per square kilometer)*

Peoples: *Over 60 separate peoples, including 23 percent Baule; 18 percent Kru; 15 percent Senufo; 11 percent Mandingo. Also 2 million people from other countries, primarily Mali, Guinea, Burkina Faso, Lebanon, and France*

Official language: *French*

Currency: *CFA franc*

National day: *National Day (December 7)*

Country's name: *The name Ivory Coast comes from the elephant ivory that used to be traded there.*

Time line:	Peoples in northern Ivory Coast region trade with people from northern Africa	Mandingo peoples settle northern region	Senufo, Kru, and Akan-speaking Abron peoples arrive	More Akan peoples settle in the east and center of region
	ca. 100 C.E.	ca. 1400	ca. 1600	ca. 1750–1800

Entertainers from the Baule people often wear masks when performing dances to honor important people in their community. This finely carved mask is made of polished wood and brass.

around 1800 to 1890, another group of Akan people, the rich, powerful Ashanti of Ghana, controlled territory in eastern Ivory Coast.

The French Take Over

Europeans were reluctant to settle in Ivory Coast because the seas were dangerous and there were no natural harbors. The first important French forts and trading posts were not built in Ivory Coast until the 1840s, when the French government paid local rulers to obtain control of some of their land.

After 1885, competition for African land between Great Britain, France, and Germany increased. France's government made more deals with local rulers and in 1893 declared that Ivory Coast was a colony of France. African peoples fought an intense war of resistance against French troops, which lasted for more than a decade. When a new French governor arrived in 1906, he imprisoned many local chiefs and introduced harsh new laws. Only in 1910 was African armed resistance finally brought to an end.

Most Africans had little education or training. There were a few missionary schools, but they taught African people that French culture and Christianity were best, encouraging them to forget their own customs and beliefs.

French farmers set up vast plantations for growing cocoa, coffee, and bananas, and they cut down large areas of rain forest for timber. They forced Africans to work the plantations and in the forests, as well as on government building projects.

By the 1940s many Ivory Coast people were striving for independence. Among their leaders was Félix Houphouët-Boigny, from the Baule people. He became leader of the Ivory Coast Democratic Party, cooperated with liberals in the French government, and became France's first black government minister.

In 1956 the French allowed their western African territories internal self-government. Houphouët-Boigny negotiated full independence from France in 1960.

Wasted Resources and Economic Problems

Compared with many other African nations, Ivory Coast was rich and had well-established trading links with Europe and elsewhere. Plantation crops fetched high prices around the world. Local

Ashanti kings of Ghana rule eastern region	France buys land in Ivory Coast	Country becomes a French colony	Ivory Coast part of French West Africa	Independence; Félix Houphouët-Boigny first president; Ivory Coast becomes one-party state
ca. 1800–1890s	**1840s**	**1893**	**1904–1958**	**1960**

people controlled many of the most profitable farms.

However, there were problems as well: Houphouët-Boigny restricted freedom of the press and political debate. He wasted vast sums on projects intended to increase his prestige, such as rebuilding his hometown, Yamoussoukro (yah-moo-SOO-kroe), and making it the capital. Senior officials lived lavishly, and the gap between rich and poor grew.

During the 1980s, prices for Ivory Coast's products fell, devastating its economy. The government was in debt, and crime levels rose as people found it hard to earn a living legally. Houphouët-Boigny introduced drastic measures to solve these problems. He canceled government projects, fired government workers, sent French experts home, and halved the amount of money cocoa farmers received when they sold their crops. As a result, in 1990 protests and strikes arose, led by students and civil servants, and the army rebelled.

Houphouët-Boigny was forced to agree to free elections, which he won. However, he died in 1993, and his successor, Henri Konan Bedie, continued Houphouët-Boigny's plans to rebuild the economy and allowed further free elections in 1995. Late in 1999, a group of army officers, led by General Robert Gueï, overthrew the government of President Bedie. They suspected that he tried to stop some opposition leaders from playing an active part in politics through plans to limit voting

rights in Ivory Coast. The new military government set up committees to review the constitution and the electoral system, and promised democratic elections for October 2000. Separate investigations into allegations of government embezzlement of overseas aid donations also started.

Today Ivory Coast faces massive foreign debt, tension between its many different peoples, and high unemployment. Coffee and cocoa exports show signs of becoming more profitable, though, and new offshore oil and gas fields may contribute to fresh economic growth.

Poor farmers work in fields near the largest Christian church in the world, the massive Basilica of Notre Dame de la Paix (Our Lady of Peace) in Yamoussoukro.

World recession causes economic crisis	Houphouët-Boigny wins first free elections	Houphouët-Boigny dies; political and economic reforms	Henri Konan Bedie elected president	Konan Bedie overthrown in coup by General Robert Gueï
1980s	**1990**	**1993**	**1995**	**1999**

Many Peoples, One Land

There are over sixty different peoples living in Ivory Coast. The majority belong to one of four main groups: the Akan-speakers, who are divided mainly into the Baule and Agni, live in the east and central regions; the Kru, who are divided mainly into the Bété (BAE-tae) and Dida (DEE-dah), live in the west; the Senufo, who live in the north; and the Mandingo, who are divided mainly into the Malinke (muh-LIHN-keh) and Dioula (JOO-lah), who also live in the north, and the Dan (DAHN), or Yacouba, who live in the far west. All these groups have different histories, lifestyles, cultural traditions, and religious customs and beliefs.

Migrants from other countries make up over 10 percent of Ivory Coast's population. Most are from other African nations, chiefly Mali, Guinea, and Burkina Faso. They

These fishermen's wives perform a dance to make sure their husbands return safely with a good catch. Customs such as this often mix elements of Christianity and African beliefs.

> ## *Blacksmith Burials*
>
> *Blacksmiths of the Senufo people are believed to have links with earth spirits, since the raw material that they work with (iron ore) comes from the earth. Because of this, they are in charge of funeral rites. When a person dies, blacksmiths carry the body through the village in a grand procession. They are accompanied by men wearing huge, frightening masks to scare away the dead person's soul. The blacksmiths dig the grave, place the body in it, and leave an offering of food. Then they hold a feast.*

came to Ivory Coast at the height of its prosperity in search of jobs, but today many are unemployed. Other settlers include French technical experts, teachers, and doctors and Lebanese, who mainly work in towns and control much of the country's wholesale trade.

The Senufo people celebrate important festivals with music and dancing. Here, a dancer wearing an animal-head mask (left) chases away another dancer dressed as a magic spirit.

French is the language used by government officials and professional people. It is also used in high schools and universities. Most ordinary people speak their own local dialect plus one of the main languages—Baule, Kru, Agni, Senufo, Mande, or Dan. Merchants and traders everywhere communicate between themselves in the Dioula language.

About six in ten people follow African religions, two in ten are Muslim, and one in ten is a Christian. In the north many Mandingo and Senufo people are Muslim; elsewhere, the Baule, the Dan, the Agni, and the Kru believe in various African religions or in Christianity. There are also many religious groups that combine Christian beliefs with African ones.

People in Ivory Coast celebrate many festivals, most having a religious origin.

Others are designed to bind communities together, to mark changes in peoples' lives, such as reaching adulthood, or to give thanks for a good harvest. Dozens of different local festivals are held throughout the year. Many include spectacular

Lo: A Secret Society

Among the Senufo people, children are prepared for adulthood by being enrolled in a secret society called the Lo. These children are taught Senufo customs and folklore and the duties they will be expected to carry out as adult members of the community. They must pass difficult tests and take part in secret rituals. Their training takes place in sacred forests and ends with special ceremonies that include music and dances with masks.

masked dancing. Muslims also observe all the main Islamic festivals.

Clans—groups of families who all trace their descent from one ancestor—play an important part in Ivory Coast society. They settle disputes, uphold customs and local laws, and bind communities together by organizing rituals and ceremonies. Most followers of African religions honor their ancestors by making offerings and performing rituals.

Health Care and Education

Although Ivory Coast has well-trained doctors and nurses and good supplies of clean water, many life-threatening infections and diseases still flourish. A large number of people, possibly over 10 percent of the population, are HIV positive or have AIDS. Most health care facilities are found only in towns and cities and the majority of people live in rural areas. Country people often rely on local healers and herbalists for help. Mission hospitals in towns and remote country areas offer free medical help to the poor. The practice of female genital cutting is widespread (see SOMALIA). An average Ivory Coast man can expect to live for about forty-five years and a woman for forty-eight.

Education is provided free by the state for the first six years of school. Only 20 percent of all students go on to high school. There are some private schools run by Roman Catholic priests and nuns, and in the northern region many boys learn to read at Koranic schools attached to local mosques. Abidjan (ah-bee-JAHN) boasts one university.

Abidjan is a busy international port. Forklift trucks load Ivory Coast goods, such as coffee and cocoa, onto big ships, which carry these products around the world.

Towns and Cities

Almost half of Ivory Coast's population lives in towns. Townspeople work in stores, offices, government departments, or food-packing and food-processing businesses. Most of the many small factories are located in the southeastern region of the country, where the largest number of people live.

One-fifth of the population lives in the largest city, Abidjan. For many years Abidjan has been famous for its style, its learning and culture, its streets lined with flowering trees, its dramatic concrete skyscrapers, its fine food, sophisticated nightlife, fashionable people, and elegant homes. Wealthy families can afford large, comfortable homes with air-conditioning, set in lush garden compounds. However, most citizens live in crowded mud and

Round houses with thatched roofs are typical of villages in Ivory Coast. Each family compound is made up of several separate houses, usually with small granaries nearby.

concrete houses built around courtyards. On the city outskirts stand slums and shantytowns, where migrants from the countryside and foreign workers live.

Other important cities include Bouaké (bwah-KAE), a trading and industrial center, and the country town of Yamoussoukro, which Houphouët-Boigny made the capital of Ivory Coast. He rebuilt it in a futuristic style with high-rise apartment and office buildings.

Villages and Farms

Away from towns and cities, people survive by farming or working on plantations. In the poorer, drier north, where the Senufo and Mandingo peoples live, farmers keep cattle and grow rice, millet, corn, cotton, and sugarcane. In the damp, warm, central rain forests, where the people are mostly Baule and Agni, farmers clear small fields to grow yams, cassava, plantains, peanuts, onions, and tomatoes. They also hunt wild animals, such as bush rat, for meat. Along the coast, where many Kru people live, fish is caught for food.

Many plantations have been established on cleared rain forest land. Most are small, owned by local farmers, and very fertile, producing bumper crops of coffee, cocoa, and cotton. Plantation owners also produce palm oil, rubber, bananas, and pineapples for export. In an average year farms and plantations produce almost four-fifths of the country's wealth.

Other rural industries include forestry and mining for diamonds, oil, gold, and iron ore. The Ivory Coast tourist industry is the most developed in western Africa, with exclusive vacation villages along the coast.

Starch and Sauce

Ivory Coast's national specialty is *attieke* (ah-tih-YEH-kae), which is steamed, grated cassava. It accompanies meat or fish cooked in a soupy stew with vegetables. This stew is known as "sauce." Similar starchy foods, such as pounded boiled yams or plantains, are called *foufou* (foo-FOO) and are served with peanut sauce or hot palm-oil sauce. In the north these starches are often replaced by rice, millet, or corn. A sauce of leaves (usually cassava leaves) is also popular. *Aloco* (uh-LOE-koe) is a favorite dish of deep-fried plantains and onions, spiced with chili. Other much-liked vegetables include eggplants, peppers, tomatoes, and okra. In towns and cities open-air restaurants called *maquis* (MAH-kee) are popular. They serve braised meats with attieke or foufou.

Locally grown pineapples, bananas, and oranges provide dessert. French-style beer

The Kru people live in southwestern Ivory Coast. On special occasions and when dancing, they wear splendid costumes decorated with beads and shells.

Frightening Masks

Baule artisans carve different kinds of wooden masks. Some are used in ceremonies commemorating an important person who has died and are beautiful, stylized portraits of the dead. Some represent naughty children; they have horns. The most dramatic are shaped like antelope or buffalo heads with gaping mouths. They represent evil spirits and are used to protect men and boys undergoing secret rituals from public view by keeping everyone else, especially women, indoors. According to Baule tradition, women who see these masks worn by dancers after dark will die.

is fashionable but expensive. Palm wine, millet beer, and a cold drink made of lemon, sugar, and ginger root are more widespread, cheaper alternatives.

Arts and Music

Ivory Coast peoples have long traditions of creative craftwork. The Senufo are famous as wood-carvers, bronze workers, and blacksmiths. They also make *korhogo* (KOER-oe-goe), a coarse, raw cotton cloth, which is painted with dramatic mud-colored designs. Originally this cloth was worn by people taking part in initiation ceremonies in a secret society or to show that they had reached adulthood. Today it is used for decorative wall hangings. Dan artisans carve wooden masks shaped like human faces for use in dancing and rituals. In some villages Baule women create pottery jugs and bowls.

Today Ivory Coast is also famous for its music. Traditional music from the north, played on large xylophones, and southern dance music, known as *gbegbe* (gih-BEHG-beh) and *polihet* (POE-lee-yeht), played on

> ## Dancers in the Forest
>
> *Until the late nineteenth century, the Dan people, who live in the remote western rain forests, had little contact with other peoples of Ivory Coast. They developed many customs and beliefs that are uniquely theirs. Some of their most famous rituals involve very athletic dancing.* Zekre touli *(ZEHK-rae TOO-lee) is performed on long stilts, sometimes over 10 feet (3 meters) high. Male dancers wear necklaces of cowrie shells, grass skirts, and masks, which are not just for disguise; they are thought to represent traditional wisdom and sometimes magic power.*
>
> Menon *(MAE-noen), a juggling dance, is performed by young girls. They leave their families at about the age of four and spend two years in secret training. Then they live with the dance groups until they are grown up and no longer take part in this dance. During the dances they are thrown into the air by male partners and perform daring dives and somersaults. In one especially skilled (and risky) dance, they land on sharp knife blades, held out by their partners high above the ground.*

guitars and accordions, are both very popular. The accordion and percussion band, Zagazougo, play Western-style tunes with African rhythms. They attract many fans, who love to dance to their fast, pounding beat. Ivory Coast's best-known singer is Alpha Blondy. His reggae music is admired around the world.

This craftsman owns a small furniture business. He is varnishing a rattan chair. Behind him more examples of his work are displayed.

KENYA

Kenya lies in eastern Africa, bordering the Indian Ocean.

Kenya's northern and northeastern regions are mainly desert. The west of the country includes the Lake Victoria Basin, part of a plateau that extends eastward to meet the Great Rift Valley. This valley, a long crack in the earth's crust, is the site of major volcanic activity. Mineral-rich lakes follow the course of the valley.

In the east, moorland, bamboo forest, and high valleys rise sharply to the jagged, snow-capped ridges of Mount Kenya, which soar to 17,058 feet (5,199 meters). Fertile farmlands descend to the rolling grasslands and tree clumps of the savanna along the Tanzanian border. A narrow fertile strip borders the beaches and coral reefs of the coast.

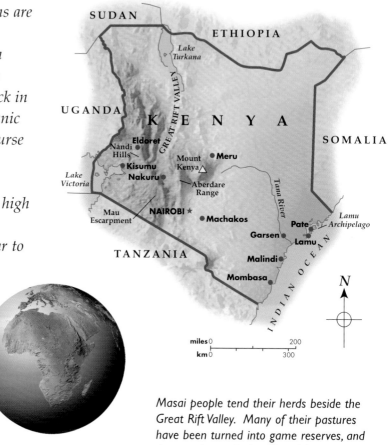

Masai people tend their herds beside the Great Rift Valley. Many of their pastures have been turned into game reserves, and they are increasingly affected by tourism.

246

Ancestors and Migrations

Early human settlement in Kenya was marked by a restless migration of peoples in search of hunting grounds, water, pasture, or farmland. Speakers of Cushitic languages arrived from the northeast between three thousand and four thousand years ago. These early settlers made pottery and well-crafted stone weapons and left behind catchments made of stone. They later mixed with the many other peoples who made Kenya their home.

Between about fifteen hundred and twenty-five hundred years ago, people from the land around the Nile River to the northwest moved into the highlands. They were speakers of Kalenjin languages. These people are the ancestors of some of today's Kalenjin-speaking peoples. At the same time speakers of Bantu languages arrived from the west and south. These people were farmers, herders, hunters, and skilled

ironworkers. They spread rapidly, and today their descendents occupy much of Kenya and make up two-thirds of the country's modern population.

When Bantu-speaking peoples reached the shores of the Indian Ocean, they mixed with earlier Cushitic-speaking settlers and also came into contact with Arab and Persian traders. These traders were Muslims who settled the islands and coasts from around the 700s C.E. onward. The

FACTS AND FIGURES

Official name: *Jamhuri ya Kenya*

Status: *Independent state*

Capital: *Nairobi*

Major towns: *Mombasa, Kisumu, Nakuru*

Area: *224,960 square miles (582,646 square kilometers)*

Population: *28,800,000*

Population density: *128 per square mile (49 per square kilometer)*

Peoples: *About 40 ethnic groups, including 21 percent Kikuyu; 14 percent Luhya; 13 percent Luo; 11 percent Kamba; 11 percent Kalenjin; 1 percent Asian, Arab, and European descent*

Official language: *Swahili*

Currency: *Kenya shilling*

National days: *Madaraka Day (June 1); Kenyatta Day (October 20); Jamhuri Day (December 12)*

Country's name: *Kenya is a version of the Kikuyu name for Mount Kenya, Kere-Nyaga or Kirinyaga, meaning "mountain of whiteness."*

CLIMATE

High altitudes keep Kenya's western and central region fairly cool. The coast is warm and humid, while the north is extremely hot and dry. The rainiest months are April and May, but in some regions a second, lesser rainy season lasts from October to December.

	Nairobi	Mombasa
Average January temperature:	65°F (18°C)	81°F (27°C)
Average July temperature:	60°F (16°C)	76°F (24°C)
Average annual precipitation:	39 in. (99 cm)	47 in. (119 cm)

Time line:	Cushitic-speaking peoples arrive from the north and east	Kalenjin and Bantu-speaking peoples arrive	Arab and Persian trading and settlement of coastal strip and islands
	2000–1000 B.C.E.	**500 B.C.E.–500 C.E.**	**700s C.E.**

The waterfront of Mombasa Island's Old Town has been a center of Indian Ocean trade and of Kenya's coastal Swahili culture for at least nine hundred years.

Bantu-speaking Africans thrived on the coast, and their rich culture, influenced by the other peoples who traded and settled there, became known as Swahili (swah-HEE-lee), which means "coastal." The Swahili culture was Islamic. Some of their coastal towns have survived and thrive today: Mombasa (mome-BAH-sah), for example, already a major port by the 1100s; Malindi (mah-LIN-dee), north of Mombasa; and Lamu (LAH-moo), an island settlement with a maze of narrow streets lined with mosques and whitewashed houses.

Other towns now lie in ruins, such as Pate, in the Lamu Archipelago, and Gedi, on the mainland close to Malindi, another ancient Swahili town that still survives. Dhows (Arabic wooden sailing ships) from the Swahili ports traded across the Indian Ocean. The Swahili controlled the export of ivory, animal skins, and farm produce, while inland peoples such as the Kamba transported goods from the interior. From the 1500s onward the Mijikenda (mih-jih-KEHN-dah) people moved toward the coast, coexisting with the Swahili.

Inland more and more peoples were entering the region. During the 1300s Masai (mah-SAI) cattle herders moved into the Rift Valley. The Masai, with the related Samburu people, displaced other tribes as they moved southward during the 1600s. This advance was finally halted in 1830 by the Hehe (HEH-hae) people in what is now Tanzania (see TANZANIA). In the 1500s, Luo (LOO-oe) people moved from southern Sudan to settle around the eastern shores of Lake Victoria, where they lived by farming and fishing. Around the same time Turkana (tuhr-KAH-nah) people moved into northeastern Kenya, around the lake that now bears their name.

Masai control Rift Valley region	Turkana occupy north; Luo move into western Kenya	Portuguese attack coast	Sultan of Zanzibar directly rules eastern African coast
1300s	**1500s**	**1505–1528**	**1720**

Europeans and Arabs

At the beginning of the sixteenth century, the first Europeans in this area, the Portuguese, sailed up the coast in search of trade and loot. They captured Mombasa in 1505 and wreaked havoc to the north and south in 1528. The Swahili towns were forced to pay tribute and their overseas trade was heavily taxed. They were also frequently raided by Portuguese troops.

By 1720 the coasts of what are now Tanzania and Kenya came under the rule of the sultans of Zanzibar (see TANZANIA). They were meant to be subordinate to the sultans of Oman, on the Persian Gulf, but it was not until the 1800s that Oman took direct command. The Omanis (oe-MAH-nees) wanted to control the spice trade. By planting large areas in the region with cloves, they increased the demand for slave labor, thereby creating a traffic in slaves that extended deep into central Africa.

In the 1880s European countries competed with each other in seizing vast areas of Africa. Kenya was desired because it lay on the overland route to the sources of the Nile River. In 1885 the European powers decreed that Kenya would be British, while Tanganyika (the mainland of modern Tanzania) would be German. The border between the two countries divided the homeland of the Masai into two halves.

The Colonial Period

The Imperial British East African Company started leasing the coastal strip of Kenya from the sultans of Zanzibar in 1887. The sultans, however, retained formal sovereignty until 1963. The British declared that the interior part of the country was a protectorate, a land under the "protection" of Great Britain, in 1895.

The timing was unfortunate for the Masai, who were quarreling among themselves. They were also suffering from cholera, and a cattle disease called rinderpest had affected their herds. The weakened Masai signed a treaty with the British invaders.

Many Kenyan peoples resisted British rule, especially the coastal Swahili and Arabs. Resistance to the British in the interior was soon subdued, and by 1903 the British were building a railroad from Mombasa on the coast westward to Lake Victoria and into Uganda.

The railroad was built by thousands of workers brought in from India, which was then part of the British Empire. They settled in Kenya and became an important part of the permanent population. An entirely new city was built on the railroad line at Nairobi (nie-ROE-bee), at the edge of the highlands. It became the new capital in 1905.

During World War I (1914–1918) about 200,000 Kenyans were servants for the British army in the fight against the German settlers in Tanganyika. Many thousands of Kenyans died of disease, malnutrition, and exhaustion.

By 1920, 20,000 Europeans, the majority of them British, had settled in the hills around Nairobi. Many set up coffee plantations. Kenyan farmers were forced off their land and into reserved areas. The

Omanis bring slaves from interior of Africa to work clove plantations	Civil war among Masai	Imperial British East African Company leases coastal strip from Sultan of Zanzibar	Great Britain claims interior as a protectorate
1800s	**1880s**	**1887**	**1895**

new Asian population also suffered racist restrictions to their civil rights. The Asians clashed with the colonial authorities and began a new period of political dissent.

The Kikuyu (kih-KOO-yoo), occupying the cool, fertile highlands, suffered greatly as the white settlers seized more and more of their prime land. A Kikuyu Central Association was founded in 1928. It campaigned for land rights, improved wages, education, and pride in Kikuyu culture. Among many matters in dispute was the practice of female genital cutting. The Kikuyu and other Bantu-speaking peoples had adopted this custom from Cushitic-speaking peoples (see SOMALIA), and it was bitterly opposed by European missionaries.

During World War II (1939–1945) the Italians who had invaded Ethiopia declared war on Kenya. Kenyan soldiers again joined up to fight, first against the Italians and then overseas. After the war they demanded justice, but they were still poorly treated and deprived of their civil rights.

In 1947 Jomo Kenyatta became leader of a political party called the Kenyan African Union (KAU), which had been founded in 1944. In 1952, as a new wave of white settlement was beginning, pent-up grievances exploded in a violent uprising. Various ethnic groups joined the struggle, but it was dominated by the Kikuyu and peoples of the central highlands. The uprising became known internationally as the Mau-Mau rebellion, possibly from the

A Kikuyu dancer wears an elaborate ceremonial headdress. Determined to retain their traditions, the Kikuyu were in the forefront of the independence movement.

muma (MOO-mah), or binding oath, sworn by the fighters. The fighters killed about one hundred white farmers in the years that followed. They also targeted their own people who would not support them. Many Kenyans were detained in British concentration camps. Others hid in the forests below Mount Kenya. By 1956 the Mau-Mau had been defeated.

Kenyatta, blamed for the uprising, was jailed from 1952 to 1959. During these years it became clear to the colonial authorities

Settlement by Indian railroad workers begins	Nairobi replaces Mombasa as capital	Kenya becomes British colony; twenty thousand white settlers arrive	Mau-Mau uprising against the British	Independence; Jomo Kenyatta elected prime minister
1903	1905	1905–1920	1952–1956	1963

that the political system would have to change. By 1960 Africans had, for the first time, achieved a majority of seats on the Legislative Council that governed the colony.

Two political parties were now formed. The Kenya African National Union (KANU) was dominated by Kikuyu and Luo members and called for a government that had strong central powers over the region. The Kenya African Democratic Union (KADU) supported a more federal form of government, in which the regions and the minority peoples had more power.

Human rights protestors publicize the torture of political prisoners by putting up posters in Nairobi. Opposition to the government has grown in recent years.

Freedom at Last

In 1963 Kenya became independent. KANU's Jomo Kenyatta had already been elected prime minister. One year later Kenya became a republic, with Kenyatta as president. KADU leaders were persuaded to join KANU, and KADU was disbanded. In 1969 KANU was the only political party to contest the elections.

Because of this lack of political strife, Kenya remained mostly peaceful and prospered. An economic union with Tanzania and Uganda, the East African Community, was attempted in 1967, but it collapsed ten years later.

Kenyatta died in 1978. His successor was Daniel arap Moi, a Kalenjin. As president, he proved to have little tolerance for opposition. Corruption and suppression of free speech increased. There were major

clashes with the Somali people in the northeast and ethnic unrest between government supporters and the mainly Kikuyu and Luo opposition.

Under international pressure, Moi was forced to hold multiparty elections in 1992. Moi and KANU won, amid claims from the opposition that the election was unfair. The Forum for the Restoration of Democracy (FORD) powerfully opposed Moi; it boycotted the 1997 election. Despite criticism of his leadership from both inside and outside Kenya, Moi succeeded once again in this contest.

Farming and Industry

The Kenyan economy is primarily based on agriculture, which employs 80 percent of the workforce. Tea and coffee are the most important export crops. They are picked in

Kenya becomes republic; Kenyatta president	Daniel arap Moi becomes president	Government troops and ethnic Somali clash	Moi and KANU win multiparty elections	Moi reelected president
1964	**1978**	**1984**	**1992**	**1997**

the central and western highlands. Large farms produce vegetables for overseas supermarket trade as well as tropical cut flowers, which are flown by airplane to the international market. Rice is grown along the Tana (TAH-nah) River, and bananas, pineapples, cashew nuts, mangoes, avocados, and coconuts are grown along the coast. In the hot and humid lands around Lake Victoria, cotton, tobacco, and sugarcane are grown. Nonfood crops include sisal, a fiber used to make rope and twine, and chrysanthemums, which are used to make pyrethrum, an insecticide.

People on small farms grow enough food for their own use. Any leftover food is sold at the local market. They grow corn, millet, barley, sorghum, and cassava, depending on the region. Most raise chickens.

Cattle are herded in most inhabited parts of the country, and dairy products and hides are exported. There is fishing in Lake Turkana and Lake Victoria and along the coast. Fish are farmed in many places.

Kenya has a wide variety of mineral resources, but few are present in commercial quantities. Calcium fluoride is mined, and salt is extracted from the lakes of the Great Rift Valley. Oil has been found in the Great Rift Valley and in the arid lands around Lake Turkana, but no commercial drilling has taken place and oil remains a major and expensive import. However, three-quarters of Kenya's energy needs are now met by hydroelectric power projects, such as those on the Tana River. The underground volcanic activity associated with the Great Rift Valley is also harnessed to create geothermal power.

Kenya's tourist industry grew very rapidly from the 1970s onward. Major attractions for the visitors, mostly Europeans, include the sandy beaches, coral reefs, and the animals found in the national parks. Such parks protect wildlife, but local people understandably resent being banned from herding cattle on land that once belonged to their ancestors. Tourism is of limited benefit to local people, since many hotels and travel companies are foreign-owned, and wages are low.

Town and Country

Kenyan society has a relatively wealthy elite and middle class, which includes expatriates, government employees, businesspeople, and many of the country's Asians. However, the great majority of people are very poor and lead a tough life,

Makeshift shacks belonging to poverty-stricken migrants edge Nairobi's suburbs. This is one side of Kenya that many tourists don't see.

working in the fields or herding. In recent years people have come to the cities in an often fruitless search for work.

Even so, over three-quarters of the population remain country dwellers. Most people live in the southern half of the country, where there are major towns and cities and a network of good roads. Many people travel by *matutu* (mah-TOO-too), the overloaded converted pickups and minibuses that noisily solicit passengers in every town. Conductors shout, whistle, and bang the sides of the vehicles until they are full.

Nairobi grew from a small colonial capital, with public buildings surrounded by streets of shops and bungalows for the white settlers, into a high-rise business center in the 1970s. The seaport of Mombasa is a very different city. It is hotter and more humid, and it has an old Swahili quarter of narrow streets as well as a modern town with tourist attractions stretching down the coast. A large Asian and Arab population lives there.

Staying the Distance

In the years before and after independence, eastern African countries arrived on the international athletics scene. In 1965 the first Kenyan long-distance superstar made his mark — twenty-five-year-old Kipchoge Keino from the Nandi Hills. He broke the world 3,000- and 5,000-meter records and went on to win four Olympic medals. Other Kenyan stars followed, including Ben Jipcho, Sabina Chebechi, Elizabeth Chelimo, and Paul Ereng in the 1970s and 1980s and Paul Tergat, Moses Kiptanui, and a host of other Kenyan long-distance champions in the 1990s.

In the arid north a Turkana woman attaches branches to hooped staves while building a new home. The Turkana people are related to both the Samburu and Masai.

Kenya has many buildings of brick and concrete, but older dwellings may still be seen. Islands such as Lamu, with whitewashed houses made of a coral cement, have preserved Swahili architecture. Houses face inward onto a courtyard. They have stone benches and elaborately carved wooden doors at the entrance. Cisterns (large stone tanks) collect rainwater. Other coastal homes are simpler rectangular buildings made of mud and stone and thatched with palm fronds. In the Kikuyu homelands round, thatched homes may be seen, while the Turkana people build domes of interwoven reeds and grasses. A Masai *manyatta* (mahn-YAH-tah), or camp, consists of homes with rounded ends. They are woven from sticks and built around the compounds where the cattle are kept. The manyatta is surrounded by a thorn stockade that protects against wild animals such as lions. More permanent settlements are villages of dried mud brick.

Everyday Life Reflects the Cultural Mix

Kenyan food is a reflection of the wide variety of ethnic groups in the country. Home cooking includes a stiff cornmeal porridge known as *ugali* (oo-GAH-lee), which is served with a sauce of vegetables or meat, often chicken or beef. Rice is also widely eaten. Vegetables include spinach,

Women prepare to cook on a small stove inside their home near Garsen, on the lower Tana River. Somali, Pokoma, and Orma peoples have settled this region.

Tasty Mandazis

You will need:

4 cardamom pods
1 egg
1 teaspoon (5 grams) baking powder
2 tablespoons (35 grams) corn oil
1 cup (.25 liters) of milk
3 tablespoons (50 grams) sugar
4 cups (1 kilogram) flour
oil for frying

Place the dry ingredients in a mixing bowl. Remove the cardamom seeds from the pod, grind them with a pestle and mortar and add to the bowl. In another bowl beat the egg and mix it with the oil. Add to the dry ingredients. Knead together, adding the milk. Allow the dough to stand for twenty minutes.

Roll out the dough to about ¹/₂ inch (1 centimeter) thick and cut into circles. Deep fry in oil for about five minutes each, until they puff up. Be very careful with hot oil; it can burn you if it spatters. This quantity serves four people.

---

carrots, and onions. *Irio* (IH-ree-oe) is a mixture of mashed potatoes, cabbage, and beans. *Mtama* (muh-TAH-mah) is a thin gruel or porridge made of millet. It is usually served for breakfast. Millet is also used to make a strong, cloudy beer.

Indian food is widely available in restaurants, and street snacks include many Indian items such as chapatis, or bread pancakes; *samozas* (sah-MOE-zahs), triangular pastry parcels of spicy meat or vegetables; and candies. Other African snacks include *mandazi* (mahn-DAH-zee), a kind of

Members of the Luo people beat drums in a funeral procession. They wear white clothes and scarves as a sign of mourning. The Luo live on the shores of Lake Victoria.

doughnut, and *mkate mayai* (mih-KAH-tee mah-YAE), or "egg bread," a pancake roll containing eggs and ground meat.

The food of coastal locations includes swordfish, prawns, coconut-flavored curries, and tropical fruits such as mangoes.

The cultural mixture of the country is also reflected in its religious buildings. Over 60 percent of the population follows Protestant or Roman Catholic Christianity. The main centers of Asian population have large mosques as well as temples for the followers of Hinduism and Jainism, two important Indian religions. Islam has ancient roots along the coast. Some mosques attract pilgrims from as far away as the Comoros. The Somali of the northeast are also Muslim.

Over one-quarter of the Kenyan population have maintained their traditional African religious beliefs. During the colonial period the Kikuyu struggled hard to preserve their beliefs amid the campaigns of Christian missionaries. The Kikuyu believe in a creator god called Ngai (ehn-GAE) and in spirits of the natural world. The earth itself is considered sacred, as are the majestic snowy peaks of Mount Kenya.

Kenyan schools offer eight years of free elementary education, and there are colleges and universities as well. Kenyans are eager to learn, but economic pressures make it hard for many young people to complete their high-school studies. Eighty-six percent of men and 70 percent of women can read and write.

Health care is available in both state-run and private hospitals and clinics. Major health problems include AIDS and malaria. Herbal medicines are still widely used in rural areas.

Peoples and Languages

Modern Kenya has about forty ethnic groups. English is widely spoken among these groups, as is Swahili, the language of the coast.

Bantu-speaking peoples make up over 66 percent of the population, of which the Kikuyu is the largest group. Based in the central highlands and the Nairobi area, many Kikuyu now run businesses or work in the capital's offices. In the days of Jomo Kenyatta, they dominated the country's political life. Many Kikuyu work on coffee plantations and farms. Women do the housework, make baskets, and tend to crops, while the men herd cattle and carry out heavier agricultural work. The Kikuyu wear Western dress except at festivals or on special occasions but have kept a strong respect for their identity and traditions. Family units are large, and the elders of the community are held in great respect. Important ceremonies mark coming-of-age, marriage, and childbirth.

Let's Talk Swahili

Swahili is a Bantu language, but it has a large number of words derived from Arabic and English. It is used on the coast and offshore islands of eastern Africa and is understood well into Uganda and central Africa.

jambo *(ZHAHM-boe)*	*hello*
kwaheri *(kwah-HAH-ree)*	*good-bye*
karibu *(kah-REE-boo)*	*welcome*
asante sana *(uh-SAHN-tee SAH-nah)*	*thank you very much*
jina lako nani? *(JEE-nah LAH-koe NAH-nee)*	*what is your name?*

The Kamba (KAHM-bah), who speak a language closely related to Kikuyu, are a large group who live in south central Kenya. They farm sorghum, millet, corn, beans, and bananas and herd cattle, sheep, and goats. Living on the northeastern shores of Lake Victoria, the Luhya (LOO-yah) make up the second largest group of Bantu-speaking peoples. They live by farming and produce fine pottery and basketry. The Gusii (GOO-see) farm the lands to the south, near the Tanzanian border. Between the Luhya and the Gusii are the Luo, who fish the eastern shores of Lake Victoria and raise cattle.

In the north are the Turkana, a people who still mostly follow a nomadic way of life and herd goats, camels, and cattle.

Wearing a headdress of feathers and buffalo horns, a healer of the Luo people examines a handful of cowrie shells to diagnose his patient's problem.

They are also hunter-gatherers and fish in Lake Turkana. Many wear traditional dress, including feathers and multiple-banded bead necklaces.

The various Kalenjin-speaking peoples of the central eastern districts are mostly farmers and laborers. Their southern neighbors are the tall thin Masai, many of whom still wear traditional dress. The women wear broad, beaded collars, headbands, and large hoop earrings. The men cut a hole in each earlobe and gradually stretch the opening by inserting plugs of increasing size. Eventually the earlobes hang in loops. They then wear beaded earrings. Masai men also wear blankets, scarlet cloaks, and carry spears or sticks to assist with herding cattle, which is their livelihood.

Masai society is grouped into clans (descendants of a common ancestor) and subdivided into age sets. For example, a boy becomes a warrior, or *moran* (moe-RAHN), at about sixteen. He paints his body with red ocher and braids his hair. In the old days he had to prove his bravery by hunting lions with spears. This age group

Tales of Past and Present

Tales of the Kenyan interior were not written down but passed on from one generation to the next by word of mouth. Many of them were wonderful fables with animals as characters. The Swahili culture has an ancient written literature, including fine love poetry. Since independence, Kenyan writers have produced a wealth of dramas, short stories, poetry, and novels.

The best-known modern author is Ngugi wa Thiongo, who was born in 1938. He first wrote in English and later in the Kikuyu language. His book Petals of Blood *described the rapid changes in a Rift Valley village after independence. Fiercely critical of the government, Thiongo was arrested in 1978. He later published his prison diaries.*

At the Eunoto ceremony, outgoing Masai warriors become elders, handing over defense of their land to a new generation. An elder spits milk from a gourd as a blessing.

Gabbra nomads, part of the Oromo group that originated in the Ethiopian highlands, move their homes by camel. Desert occupies most of the northern half of Kenya.

has always been chiefly responsible for cattle herding. Later age-sets are marked by marriage and becoming a respected elder of the tribe. Once living mostly on milk and cow's blood, the Masai diet today is more diverse, including corn and goat and sheep meat.

The ethnic groups of the northeastern deserts are dominated by the Somali (soe-MAH-lee), nomadic herders of goats.

The Game of Bao

Bao (BAH-oe) is the Swahili word for a board game for two people played widely across Africa. North American children often play one version of the game called Mankala. Boards may be made from beautifully carved wood or simply from scoops scratched in the soil. The rules of this very complex game vary, but in Kenya and Tanzania there are normally sixty-four pieces and four rows of eight scoops. The aim is to capture your opponent's pieces. The game is mostly played by adult males, and there is a lot of prestige to be won if skillful at playing.

Theirs is a male-dominated society, with men being allowed to take several wives. They are part of a larger ethnic group that stretches northward into Somalia itself and on to Djibouti (see SOMALIA and DJIBOUTI). Somali groups have often been accused of being bandits by the Kenyan authorities, and many armed conflicts have arisen in this region.

The Borana (buh-RAH-nah) live as herders of camels and cattle in the north. They are related to the Oromo people of Ethiopia (see ETHIOPIA).

The coastal peoples include the Mijikenda peoples. They work as farmers, fishers, market traders, and laborers. The men mostly wear Western dress. Boldly patterned sarongs and head scarves are popular with the women.

The Mijikenda coexist with the peoples of the Swahili tradition. As strict Muslims, Swahili women wear black dresses and a black veil called *buibui* (boo-ee-BOO-ee) in public places. However, in their homes, in the company of other women during feasts such as weddings, colorful dresses may

For a Swahili wedding the bride's hands and wrists are painted with henna in designs as intricate as lace. This custom arrived in eastern Africa with Arab settlers.

Sounds of Eastern Africa

Kenya has an ancient tradition of music, dance, and drumming. The classical Kikuyu instrument is the *gicandi* (jih-KAHN-dee), a gourd used like maracas. Luhya musicians play an eight-stringed lyre and flutes. The *tarab* (tah-RAHB) music of Swahili weddings and festivals has an Arabic sound and soulful lyrics; many of its finest singers are women. Modern African pop music has broken down national frontiers, with both Tanzanian and Congolese bands being hugely popular in Kenya. However, the guitar style called *benga* (BEHN-gah), which became popular in Kenya in the 1970s and 1980s, was clearly influenced by traditional Luo stringed instruments.

replace black robes. Men wear a cotton kilt wrapped around the waist and a small embroidered cap, or *koffia* (koe-FEE-ah). Swahili crafts include making intricate carvings in wood and building wooden ships. The great days of trade up to Arabia and across to India, making use of the rain-bearing monsoon winds, have largely passed, but many ships with triangular sails in the Arabic dhow style still sail the coast of eastern Africa down to Zanzibar. However, the larger ocean-going dhows are rarely built anymore.

Kenya's Asian community is mainly involved in business, commerce, tourism, catering, and communications. It maintains close links with other Asian communities in Tanzania and Uganda. The European community consists mostly of British farming families who stayed on after independence and have become Kenyan citizens. Many recent European arrivals work in the offices and embassies of Nairobi.

Musicians assemble for the Maulidi procession on the Lamu waterfront. This annual Islamic festival celebrates the birth of Muhammad, the founder of Islam.

LESOTHO

LESOTHO IS A SMALL, MOUNTAINOUS LANDLOCKED COUNTRY completely surrounded by South Africa.

All of Lesotho is more than 3,200 feet (1,000 meters) above sea level. The rugged Maluti Mountains, part of the Drakensberg Range, cover roughly two-thirds of the country. They include Thabana Ntlenyana, the highest peak in southern Africa at 11,425 feet (3,482 meters). The remaining third of the country is called the "lowlands," although the land is still high. These lowlands form a 25-mile- (40-kilometer-) wide corridor along the eastern side of the Caledon River. This is where the best agricultural land can be found and where most people live.

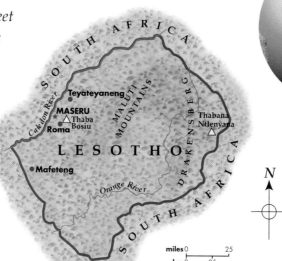

Using a sled is a good way of transporting cattle fodder in this rugged country. Raising crops is difficult in Lesotho, but cattle thrive and are one of the country's main exports.

CLIMATE

Lesotho has a temperate climate. Most rainfall occurs between October and April. In the mountains, which are frequently snow covered, frosts can occur at any time.

Average January temperature: *68°F (20°C)*
Average July temperature: *50°F (10°C)*
Average annual precipitation: *28 in. (71 cm)*

The Building of a Nation

Cave paintings reveal some information about the San (SAHN) people who lived in the rock shelters of the Lesotho (luh-SOE-toe) region thousands of years ago. They ate mostly fruit, nuts, and insects and hunted wild animals using poisoned arrows. Most either intermarried with or were displaced by Bantu-speakers, who began arriving in southern Africa around 200 C.E.

Bantu (BAN-too) farmers were living in the Lesotho region by about 1000 C.E. They were the Sotho (SOE-toe) people, who lived peacefully in small chiefdoms for hundreds of years. Then in the 1820s all of southern Africa was caught up in a series of wars triggered by the expansion of the Zulu kingdom located east of the Drakensberg (DRAH-kuhnz-buhrk) Range. Groups fleeing from the Zulu destroyed chiefdoms, and the Sotho people were scattered. Many peoples sought refuge at Thaba Bosiu, a flat-topped mountain from where Moshoeshoe I, the king of a Sotho group called the Kwena, skillfully defended the Sotho peoples.

By the 1830s Moshoeshoe had molded the powerful Basuto kingdom out of the various Sotho chiefdoms and refugees in the area. The kingdom, including highlands and lowlands, was about double the size of present-day Lesotho. From the 1830s onward, however, the Sotho faced a new threat from Afrikaner (Dutch) farmers, who had moved inland to get away from British rule in Cape Colony (see SOUTH AFRICA). As the Afrikaners seized land in the fertile lowlands, the Sotho fought them in a series of defensive wars through the 1850s and 1860s. Moshoeshoe continually appealed to the British for help and protection. When the British finally declared a protectorate over the area they called Basutoland, most of the fertile Caledon (KA-luh-duhn) Valley had been lost to the Afrikaners, and the present mountainous kingdom was all that

FACTS AND FIGURES

Official name: *Kingdom of Lesotho*

Status: *Independent state*

Capital: *Maseru*

Major towns: *Teyateyaneng, Mafeteng*

Area: *11,716 square miles (30,344 square kilometers)*

Population: *2,100,000*

Population density: *179 per square mile (69 per square kilometer)*

Peoples: *Almost all Sotho; a few thousand Asians and Europeans*

Official languages: *English and Sesotho*

Currency: *Loti*

National days: *Moshoeshoe Day (March 11); Heroes' Day (April 4); King's Birthday (July 17); Independence Day (October 4)*

Country's name: *It is named after the Sotho people, the country's main ethnic group.*

remained. Moshoeshoe died in 1870, having at least secured the remnants of his kingdom.

British attempts to impose a tax on African homes and to take away the guns of the Sotho chiefs led to the Gun War of 1880–1881. The Sotho defeated British military expeditions sent from the Cape and forced the British to make concessions to secure a cease-fire. Most important, the British agreed to administer Basutoland separately from the Cape. When the Union of South Africa was formed in 1910, Basutoland remained under British rule, but was administered from South Africa.

Time line:	Khoisan-speakers living in southern Africa	Bantu-speakers move into region	Sotho base established at Thaba Bosiu	Sotho people fight wars against Afrikaners	British declare protectorate of Basutoland
	ca. 18,000 B.C.E.	ca. 200–1000 C.E.	1824	1850s–1860s	1868

This man is one of the many Sotho who work in neighboring South Africa. The money he sends home is essential for his family's survival.

The Move toward Independence

During the 1930s young people were increasingly critical of British rule and impatient with the chiefs' authority. The British introduced reforms that reduced the power and number of the chiefs, and spent little on health and education. The first political parties were formed in the 1950s, and during the following decade British colonies in Africa moved toward independence. The first elections were held under a new constitution in 1965 and were won by the Basutoland National Party (BNP), which was led by Chief Joseph Leabua Jonathan. The king, Moshoeshoe II, was head of state but had few powers. The country became independent in 1966.

Fearful of defeat by the Basotho Congress Party (BCP) in the election of 1970, the BNP staged a coup and then held power until 1986. During the 1970s, Chief Jonathan showed an increasingly hostile attitude toward the racist policies of South Africa. This prompted the South African army to raid Maseru (MA-zuh-roo) for South African political refugees in 1982. The South African government also restricted the movement of goods and people across the border.

In 1986 Major-General Justin Lekhanya led a coup backed by South Africa. He established a military council and expelled South African political refugees from Lesotho. Political change in South Africa led to the overthrow of Lekhanya by Colonel Elias Ramaena in 1991. Ramaena lifted the ban on political parties. New free elections were held in May 1993, and the Basotho Congress Party won all the seats. When the BCP won all the seats again in 1998, there was widespread suspicion of vote rigging. Antigovernment demonstrations became violent, and the king, Letsie III, called for assistance from South Africa. Lesotho's troops and demonstrators, however, saw South African intervention as a foreign invasion, and in the violent clash that followed much of the capital, Maseru, was damaged or destroyed. This destruction has set back Lesotho's economic development, and the country's political future remains tense and uncertain.

Gun War	Independence; country renamed Lesotho	Justin Lekhanya seizes power	Elias Ramaena overthrows Lekhanya	Elections bring Basotho Congress Party to power	Elections and violence; South Africa intervenes
1880–1881	1966	1986	1991	1993	1998

Lesotho Today

Almost all the people of Lesotho are Sesotho-speakers, with subgroups including Kwena (KWAE-nah), Nguni (uhn-GOO-nee), and Mahlape (mah-LAH-pae). A few thousand Asians and Europeans also live in Lesotho.

Lesotho is an overwhelmingly Christian country; missionaries were welcomed in the nineteenth century. Today about one-quarter of the people are followers of the Lesotho Evangelical Church, and around 40 percent are Roman Catholic. Some 11 percent are Anglican, and the rest belong to other Christian denominations or follow traditional religions.

The churches in Lesotho produce many religious and educational publications and books on Sesotho literature and language, which have helped to preserve Sotho folklore. Mission schools taught people how to read and write. The effect of this education can be seen in the relatively high literacy rate for African nations: 71 percent of Lesotho's adult population can read and write. Most children go to elementary schools, which are often run by the churches. However, only about one-quarter go on to secondary schools. There is a university at Roma.

The people of Lesotho suffer from malnutrition and diseases related to the rigors of the climate, with rheumatism and respiratory diseases common. Health facilities are concentrated in the lowland urban areas, with few facilities or medical staff in the countryside.

In the lowlands tarred roads run along Lesotho's western and southern borders. Gravel roads cut through the mountains,

Lesotho's health workers have difficulty reaching sick people who live in remote mountainous country. Here, nurses use motorbikes for their home visits.

but the extremely remote mountain villages can only be reached on foot and horseback and by four-wheel-drive vehicles.

Most people try to make their living from the land. In the 10 percent of the country where cultivation is possible, crops include wheat, sorghum, rice, corn, fruits, and vegetables. People also attempt to grow crops on hill slopes. While this land makes good pasture for sheep and cattle, the cultivation of crops has resulted in serious erosion. Higher up, overgrazing has caused the loss of grass cover. Cattle, together with wool and mohair from the sheep, form the country's main exports.

Often the only way in which families can survive is for the men to go to work in South African mines. More than one-third of Lesotho's active men are such migrant workers. The money they send back to their families is the most important source of income in the country and is essential for the stability of Lesotho's economy. Many smaller towns in Lesotho are camps for migrant workers on their way to and from South Africa.

There are diamonds in Lesotho, but the main mine was closed in 1982 due to a fall in world demand. Manufacturing industries are small and are concentrated around Maseru. They include food processing, textiles, clothes, furniture making, and ceramics.

The Lesotho Highlands Water Project, scheduled to be completed in 2015, is likely to bring substantial benefits to the country's economy. The headwaters of the Orange River, which rise high in the Maluti Mountains, are being dammed. The vast amounts of water collected will be piped and sold to the industrial regions of South Africa, and a hydroelectric project will provide all the energy Lesotho needs.

Life of the People

Maseru is the only town of considerable size in Lesotho; it has a modern center, which was partially damaged by South African troops in 1998. The population of Maseru is increasing rapidly because people come to the town

These women are receiving bags of grain for their families. Much of the land in Lesotho is poor and unsuitable for cultivation, and some people depend on international food aid for their survival.

264

Ponies and Blankets

Ponies and blankets were introduced in Lesotho in the nineteenth century. King Moshoeshoe I brought ponies from the Cape region of southern Africa in 1829. He soon learned to ride and quickly introduced more ponies into the kingdom. By the time of his death, the Sotho people had mastered riding their sturdy ponies along the steep and rugged mountain paths.

European traders introduced blankets in the 1860s. The Sotho people quickly adopted them, finding them very practical wear for a cold climate. They are fastened around the shoulders with a large safety pin. Although the blankets are made in South Africa, they have become part of Lesotho culture. For example, young women wear blankets around their hips until they have their first child.

Living in the mountains, this man finds his pony the best way to get around. He wears a decorated wool blanket and a conical hat made from reeds.

looking for work, and shantytown settlements line its outskirts.

The traditional Sotho way of life extends to rural areas. A group of about five extended families, maybe thirty households, makes up a village. The houses are circular or rectangular and are made of turf, clay, or stone. In the past they all had thatched roofs, but grooved iron roofs are now common. At the village's center stands the chief's house. The chief is the highest authority in the village, and many village disputes are settled in his court.

Village life changes with the seasons. Migrant workers try to return home to help with plowing and harvest, but mostly it is the women and girls who work in the fields, while the boys look after the sheep, cattle, and goats on the hillsides. When herding animals, men and boys sometimes play a *lesiba* (leh-SEE-bah), a string stretched between the ends of a long stick. Blowing across the string produces imitation bird sounds; these noises help to control the cattle.

Using natural dyes, village people decorate their houses with patterns. They make pots and weave grass mats and conical reed hats. Tourists buy these hats as well as wool mats and tapestries.

LIBERIA

LIBERIA IS A SMALL COUNTRY lying on the
coast of western Africa.

*Lagoons and mangrove swamps fringe
Liberia's coastline. These give way to a
gently rolling plain. Further inland
stand dense tropical forests, which lead to
low mountains in the north and east. The
highest point is Mount Wutivi at 4,000 feet
(1,220 meters). The land is well fed by its
rivers, which flow parallel to each other, from
the mountains to the Atlantic Ocean.*

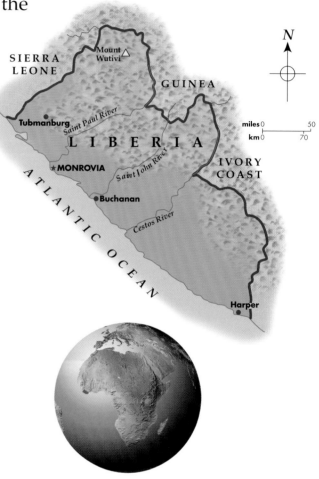

CLIMATE

*Liberia is hot and humid for much of the year.
There are two rainy seasons: one from May to
July and the other from September to November.
Rainfall is heavier near the coast. During
December and January a dry wind blows in from
the Sahara Desert, covering the land with sand
and dust.*

Average January temperature: *79°F (26°C)*

Average July temperature: *76°F (24°C)*

Average annual precipitation:
   on the coast: *177 in. (450 cm)*
   inland: *69 in. (175 cm)*

*Liberian children raise their national flag. The single star and
the horizontal red and white stripes clearly show that the
design is based on the U.S. flag.*

Forest Isolation and Coastal Traders

There are no written records
about the early history of the
Liberian coastal and forest
peoples. The earliest peoples
were likely to have been
hunter-gatherers who lived by
hunting animals, gathering
wild berries and vegetables,
and catching fish in the sea and
in local rivers.

For a long time the thick forests and mountains of Liberia (lie-BIR-ee-uh) kept its peoples isolated from each other and from the powerful states of the western African savanna. Trading links with these states probably began about one thousand years ago. Peoples of Liberia who spoke languages of a family called Mande formed strong cultural links with other Mande-speaking people who dominated the Mali Empire in the western Sahel region between the thirteenth and sixteenth centuries. These links also helped spread ideas on farming. The coastal and forest peoples began to live in small villages, cultivating yams and rice and keeping domestic animals. They traded in sea salt and dried fish. Most people lived in small communities, some lived in small states. They passed down their history orally through storytelling, music, and dance.

The Portuguese were the first Europeans to sail around the coast of western Africa in the fifteenth century. They began to trade with the coastal peoples, selling cheap iron, cloth, copper, and guns in exchange for goods such as ivory, gold, and pepper. They—and other Europeans, such as the Dutch, British, and French—soon began to buy people as well. They wanted slaves to work on their new sugar and tobacco plantations in the Americas.

The arrival of Europeans encouraged peoples such as the Vai (VAE), and later the Mandingo (mahn-DIHN-goe), to migrate to the coast to take control of profitable trade opportunities. By the end of the eighteenth century, many previously peaceful villages

FACTS AND FIGURES

Official name: Republic of Liberia

Status: Independent state

Capital: Monrovia

Major towns: Buchanan, Harper, Tubmanburg

Area: 43,000 square miles (111,370 square kilometers)

Population: 2,900,000

Population density: 67 per square mile (26 per square kilometer)

Peoples: 20 percent Kpelle; 14 percent Bassa; 14 smaller indigenous ethnic groups, including the Gio, Gola, Grebo, Kru, Loma, Mandingo, Mano, Vai; also Americo-Liberians

Official language: English

Currency: American dollar and Liberian dollar

National day: Independence Day (July 26)

Country's name: Liberia comes from the Latin liber, meaning "free."

had erected defenses because of the fear of slave raids and military invasion by new settlers from the north.

Freed Slaves Arrive from America

In nineteenth-century America, many states still allowed slavery, but there were also freed slaves, the descendants of the millions of Africans captured and shipped across the Atlantic. Freedom did little to improve their lives, and most were treated as second-class citizens. In 1816 a group of white Americans founded the American

Time line:

ca. 1000 C.E.	1400s
Trading contacts established with savanna states in western Africa; people settle in small villages and farms	Portuguese arrive on west African coast and begin trading; peoples start migrating from north to coast

267

Colonization Society with the aim of resettling freed slaves in Africa.

In 1821 a group of black settlers arrived on the coast and established the settlement of Monrovia (named after U.S. President James Monroe). Between 1821 and 1865, fifteen thousand settlers arrived and the colony of Liberia was born. The early settlers experienced troubled times; the death rate was high because few had immunity to local diseases, particularly malaria. There were frequently conflicts with the indigenous African peoples, who often attacked the new settlements.

At first Liberia was ruled by white governors, and the black settlers had little say in government. The black settlers demanded—and won—their independence in 1847. The first president was Joseph Roberts, a mulatto. Mulattos were of mixed black and white parentage, and during the first years of independence they dominated the government of Liberia. Liberia modeled its republican constitution, its education system, and its religious practices on those in the United States.

Gradually power shifted to the black settlers. Their party, the True Whig Party, came to power in 1877 and held on to power until 1980.

Liberia in the Twentieth Century

During the early years of the twentieth century, rubber production from plantations owned by the American Firestone Tire and Rubber Company dominated the economy. Firestone helped finance the Americo-

> ## *Benjamin Anderson: Explorer*
>
> *Benjamin Anderson was an Americo-Liberian born in Liberia. He should be famous as one of the great explorers of Africa but remains virtually unknown.*
>
> *In 1868 he spent a year traveling in the remote regions of western Africa, carefully mapping out a large area. Unlike many travelers, he recorded what he actually saw and did not embellish his writings with stories of murderous chiefs and cannibal tribes. He did not hold the common white view that the "natives" were inferior and needed civilizing. On the whole he was treated kindly. He observed that most of the stories of terrible tyrant chiefs were actually spread by the chiefs themselves to inspire fear and respect from their people and from other tribes.*

Liberian government in its efforts to expand into areas where wild rubber grew. Firestone and the government also worked together to force the rural indigenous peoples of the region to become workers on the developing plantations.

William Tubman was president of Liberia from 1944 to 1971. Tubman urged indigenous Liberians to take part in government, expanded education, and encouraged investment from overseas. But the vast majority of Liberians, especially those in the interior, remained extremely

Height of transatlantic slave trade	Black settlers arrive from United States and establish Monrovia	Liberia becomes independent state	Mulattos dominate government
1600s–mid 1800s	1821	1847	1847–1877

A worker on a Liberian rubber plantation taps a rubber tree. He cuts into the bark and a milky white liquid, known as latex, seeps from the tree.

close to collapse. From 1989 to 1996 Liberia descended into a terrible civil war. Doe's government was overthrown and he was killed in 1990. Tribal-based militias fought to control the country. Eventually the different factions, aided by a peacekeeping force from different western African countries, agreed to peace.

Open elections were held in 1997, and Charles Taylor became president. Peace has been restored, but Liberia remains unstable, and its economy is in near ruins. It has been estimated that nearly 10 percent of Liberia's peoples died in the civil war and that more than 80 percent are refugees, either displaced from their villages within Liberia or having fled across the borders into neighboring countries.

poor and excluded from power. This, and the corruption and flamboyant wealth of those at the top, led to increasing resentment and opposition.

Tubman's successor, William Tolbert Jr., was killed in 1980 in a military coup led by Samuel Doe, a junior officer in the Liberian army. Doe became the first head of state who was an indigenous Liberian. In 1985 elections were held, from which opposition parties were barred, and Doe became president of a new civilian government. During his years of power, the economy was badly managed, corruption increased greatly, and those who opposed his rule were brutally suppressed.

Opposition grew as repression increased, and the economy came

Women and babies receive food at a feeding center. Liberians who became refugees in their own country during the civil war could not grow or buy food for their families.

True Whig Party, the party of the black settlers, controls Liberia	Military coup led by Samuel Doe overthrows government of William Tolbert	Doe's government overthrown; civil war	Open elections held; Charles Taylor elected president
1877–1980	**1980**	**1989–1996**	**1997**

Ethnic Groups and Religions

The Republic of Liberia has sixteen indigenous ethnic groups that make up 95 percent of the population. Each ethnic group speaks its own language. The largest ethnic groups are the Kpelle (kih-PEH-lee) and the Bassa (BAH-sah), who make up one-fifth and one-seventh of the population respectively. Other major ethnic groups include the Gio (or Dan), the Gola, the Grebo, the Kru, the Loma (or Toma), the Mandingo, the Mano, and the Vai.

The other 5 percent are Americo-Liberians, descendants of the black American settlers from the nineteenth century. English is the language of the Americo-Liberians and is also the national language. During the early decades of Americo-Liberian rule, a pidgin English developed along the coast. It used English words with local African structures and was used as a means of communication between Americo-Liberians and indigenous peoples.

Liberia is officially a Christian country, reflecting the faith of the first black settlers from the United States. Many Liberians also follow African religions and Islam. Statistics vary greatly as to the numbers following a particular religion; some state that the majority are Christians, others that the majority follow African religions. It is difficult to give accurate figures about people's religious beliefs because people often mix their religions. Many who are Christian or Muslim may well continue to follow some of the religious practices of their African ancestors.

The followers of African religions share belief in a supreme God who created everything on the earth. Their beliefs and practices vary, but almost all believe that because God is all-powerful, humans cannot communicate with or worship him directly, but through spirits and the natural world. Ancestors are an important link with God because they are closer to God than the living. Yet most Liberians believe their ancestors are still present in everyday life and should be shown special respect.

The Poro

The Poro (POE-roe) are secret societies found in the Liberian interior. They have declined in importance with the spread of Christianity and Islam and increasing Westernization.

The Poro societies hand down the traditions and culture of a community or ethnic group from one generation to the next. One important function of the Poro is to initiate boys—and girls, whose societies are known as Sande (SHAHN-dee)—into adulthood. During the initiation ceremony the boys have to live rough in the bush and are taught the customs and laws of their community. They have to face tests of their physical courage. The final test is when they face the terrifying masked Poro spirit. This symbolizes rebirth: the child is "swallowed" by the Poro spirit. When he returns to his family, he is reborn as a man.

The Poro also plays an important part in keeping law and order in the community. All Poro members are sworn to absolute secrecy and appear as masked spirits on special occasions. They are believed to hold religious secrets and to be able to communicate with the Poro spirit through its shrines. Anyone who commits a crime or behaves badly in the community is brought before the Poro members for punishment.

Civil War Affects Education, Health, and Economy

Education in Liberia is free, and all children between the ages of six and sixteen are required to attend. In reality, however, less than half of Liberia's children go to school. This is partly because of a shortage of money to build and run schools, partly because there is a shortage of trained teachers, and in recent years, because of the disruption to normal life caused by the civil war. Most schools used to be run by Christian missions, but almost all are now government run.

Health facilities, including local clinics and hospitals, are unevenly spread in Liberia, with better facilities in the capital. Life expectancy normally averages fifty-

Children being taught at a displaced persons' camp. Facilities are very limited, but classes here help children continue their education until it is safe to return to their village schools.

nine years. The effects of the civil war have been devastating on the health of much of the population. Existing facilities have simply not been able to cope with the flood of injured civilians and the illnesses caused by unclean water supplies and lack of food.

Liberia has plenty of water and favorable conditions for agriculture. Most Liberians are farmers, producing enough food for their family, with maybe a little left to sell at market. Cash crops, such as rubber, are grown on large plantations. With more than 300 miles (480 kilometers) of coastline, fishing has always been important. Other natural resources, such as minerals and large areas of forest, could be developed. Iron ore is mined, but there is little industry.

One unusual area from which Liberia receives income is from the registration of foreign ships. Ships pay to fly the Liberian "flag of convenience" instead of the flag of their own country. In this way they do not

have to pay any taxes or follow the shipping rules set by their own government.

Today Liberia has huge foreign debts and the civil war has almost destroyed the economy. Many businesspeople have fled the country.

Rural Life and Culture

In rural areas most Liberians live by farming. The forest that covers large swaths of the interior has always determined the way people live. They clear land on the forest fringes to plant crops. Every few years the soil becomes exhausted, and they must clear new land. Villages are normally compact, and the houses are either circular or rectangular. They have thatched roofs or, if the family can afford it, a zinc roof.

Music and dance have always been at the heart of Liberian village life. Liberians will dance and sing at every opportunity—for weddings and funerals, to celebrate ancestors, when important visitors come,

and when they simply feel like singing and dancing. Many play different instruments, including drums, harplike instruments, and rattles made from gourds. The most popular drum is held under the arm and squeezed. Different movements vary the tone of the drum.

Liberian villages have been able to meet many basic needs. Village crafts supply essentials: the weaver and the tailor make clothes and the blacksmith makes tools for farming and for home use. Regular open markets allow people to sell and to buy produce.

During the rainy season, river flooding often means that villages become cut off from the markets, neighboring villages, and sometimes even their own farmland. During these times, precarious suspension bridges, which are made by hand from materials cut from the forest, are the only

Hope for the future: families return to their villages and begin rebuilding their lives. Here women work together to grow crops on land damaged by fighting during the civil war.

Liberians in downtown Monrovia. The simple necessities of everyday life are beginning to replace the guns and soldiers of the civil war on the streets.

way that villagers can get around to carry on a normal life.

For most Liberians the staple food is rice. Many families will eat rice twice a day if it is available and affordable. They also eat cassava, sweet potatoes, and yams. To these foods they will add various hot peppery sauces, which may contain meat or fish. Green vegetables are frequently used in Liberian sauces, including okra, spinach and cabbage. Green tops of potatoes and cassava are also used, and peanuts are a popular addition to different sauces.

The civil war has taken a terrible toll on the rural communities of Liberia. Whole villages were destroyed, and thousands of people fled into the bush or onto the highways in a desperate search for food and shelter. In small ways rural Liberians are now attempting to rebuild their communities. Projects have been started to get food production going again, schools repaired, and health clinics reopened.

Monrovia: High-Rises and Shacks

The only major town in Liberia is Monrovia, the capital and chief port. The population today is estimated to be nearly one million, including refugees from rural Liberia. Monrovia is a city of contrasts, with stone houses in the style of the grand houses of the U.S. South and modern high-rise offices alongside shacks built by the poor.

During the years of the civil war, Monrovians' lives were torn apart. There was no electricity, little clean water, and little food. Soldiers—often boys not yet in their teens—roamed the streets, brandishing machine guns and preventing people from leaving their homes and refugee camps. After six years the night curfew in Monrovia was finally lifted in 1998.

LIBYA

LIBYA IS A NATION IN NORTHERN AFRICA, the fourth largest country on the continent. Its long northern coastline adjoins the Mediterranean Sea.

The northwest consists of a marshy coastal strip edging the flat Al-Jifarah Plain, with the rugged Nafusah Plateau immediately to the south. The northeast consists of the narrow Al-Marj Plain along the coast, with the Al-Akhdar Mountains immediately inland. The rest of the country is part of the vast Sahara Desert. The Tibesti Mountains lie in the far south; Bikku Bitti Peak rises to 7,436 feet (2,266 meters).

Libya has no permanent rivers, only dry watercourses, called wadis, that fill up and flow for a short time after occasional heavy rains. Along the coast just enough rain falls for Mediterranean shrubs and trees to grow.

CLIMATE

Coastal areas experience dry, sunny summers, frost-free winters, and light rainfall from October to February. In the desert, temperatures can rise to 122°F (50°C) at noon and fall to freezing after dark. Dust storms and sandstorms are frequent, and often no rain falls for years at a time. A hot, dry desert wind called the ghibli blows northward toward the coast in spring and autumn, scorching people and damaging crops.

Average January temperature: *46°F (8°C)*

Average July temperature: *86°F (30°C)*

Average annual precipitation: *15 in. (38 cm)*

Libyans harvest barley in fields at the desert's edge. Libya's hot, dry climate makes it impossible to grow enough food for everyone. Therefore, most food is imported.

A Home for Many Peoples

The first traces of modern human settlement in northern Africa date from around 50,000 B.C.E. In Libya widespread evidence of human activity, such as stone tools and arrowheads, survives from around 25,000 B.C.E. At that time the Sahara was not a desert; it began to dry up around 5000 B.C.E. People living there moved to settle along its northern edges or at scattered oases.

From around 1500 to 400 B.C.E., a people known as the Garamantians (gah-rah-MAHN-tee-uhns) lived in Libya and made contact and traded with the mighty Egyptian civilization to the east. The Garamantians kept horses, drove chariots, and hunted wild animals such as deer and gazelle in the desert. Examples of the beautiful rock paintings they created survive on cliffs and in caves. Between around 1000 B.C.E. and 500 C.E., other powerful nearby civilizations established colonies on Libyan land: first the Phoenicians from the eastern Mediterranean, then the Greeks, then the Romans.

Around 100 C.E camels were introduced to northern Africa from the Middle East. Camels can survive for days without fresh food or water. This made it easier to go on long journeys across the Sahara. Long-distance trade became more frequent, linking Tripoli (TRIH-puh-lee) on the Libyan coast with cities and kingdoms in present-day Algeria, Mali, and Chad.

During the seventh century Muslim armies from Arabia and the Middle East took control of northern Africa and introduced a new faith, Islam. The native Berber (BUHR-buhr) people became Muslims; over the next five hundred years, more Muslim settlers arrived from Arab lands. They married local people, and it is from these marriages that most Libyans are descended today.

FACTS AND FIGURES

Official name: Al Jumahiriyah al Arabiyah al Libiyah ash Shabiyah al Ishtirakiyah (Socialist People's Libyan Arab Jamahiriya)

Status: Independent state

Capital: Tripoli

Major towns: Benghazi, Misratah

Area: 679,358 square miles (1,759,537 square kilometers)

Population: 5,000,000

Population density: 7 per square mile (3 per square kilometer)

Peoples: 90 percent mixed Arab-Berber; 4 percent Berber and Tuareg; 3 percent Harratin; also Tebu and many workers from overseas

Official language: Arabic

Currency: Libyan dinar

National days: Declaration of the Jamahiriya—People's State (March 2); Evacuation of the Foreign Military Bases (June 11); Revolution Day (September 1); Day of Mourning (October 26); Independence Day (December 24)

Country's name: Libya was the Roman name for eastern North Africa; Jamahiriya means "People's State" or "State of the Masses."

Time line:	First humans in northern Africa	Late Stone Age technologies in use	Sahara drying up; Libya becoming desert	Powerful Garamantian Empire; links with Egypt
	50,000 B.C.E.	**ca. 25,000 B.C.E.**	**ca. 5000–2000 B.C.E.**	**ca. 1500–400 B.C.E.**

Roman Remains

The ruins of Greek and Roman cities can be found close to the Mediterranean coast. The most famous is Leptis Magna. Its finest buildings date from the reign of the Roman Emperor Lucius Septimius Severus, who was Libyan; he ruled from 193 to 211 C.E. Almost eighty thousand people lived in Leptis at that time. They would have enjoyed strolling across the vast forum (main market square), watching plays at the theater, or going to chariot races and animal fights in the arena. They exercised in the palestra *(pah-LAE-strah), a sports center, or enjoyed a sauna and swim at the public baths. There was a harbor with a lighthouse, several temples, grand government buildings, and huge, decorated triumphal arches that were built to celebrate the power of emperors and army generals in Rome. Today the remains of all these buildings can be seen.*

In 1510 Spanish Christian princes conquered Tripoli. Spanish control did not last long, however. In 1551 the Ottoman Turks, based in Istanbul, conquered all of Libya and ruled it until 1711, when Libya's ports were captured by a dynasty of pirates, the Karamanlis. In 1835 the Ottomans defeated the Karamanlis and ruled Libya again until 1911. For most of the nineteenth century, Libyan tribal leaders demanded independence from Ottoman rule. After 1843 these were headed by members of the Sanusi family, leaders of a Muslim religious revival movement.

Besides facing Sanusi demands for independence, the Ottomans were attacked by European powers. In 1911 Italy seized Libya. The Libyan people fought fiercely against Italian rule. From 1923 to 1931, guerrilla forces fought against the Italians. After this, Libyan resistance to the Italians faded away, and Libya became a colony of Italy in 1934. For the next ten years, Italian colonial rulers treated the Libyans cruelly. Almost half the Libyan population was exiled or killed, and the best farmland was given to Italian settlers.

Freedom Followed by Controversy

During World War II (1939–1945), Libya became a battlefield as British troops and the Sanusi movement fought the Italians and the Germans. In 1947 Italy agreed to surrender control of Libya to the United Nations, which granted independence to Libya in 1952. The Sanusi leader became King Idris I.

At this time Libya was still very poor. Then in the late 1950s oil was discovered in enormous quantities. But the oil drilling and exporting companies were all foreign-owned, which meant most of the profits left the country. By 1969 the government was criticized for not making the best use of Libya's oil. In a bloodless revolution Colonel Mu'ammar Gadhafi, a twenty-seven-year-old army officer, forced the king

Phoenician, Greek, Roman colonies in Libya	Arab conquerors bring Islam to Libya	Arabs migrate from Arabia and Egypt into Libya	Ottomans rule Libya	Karamanli pirates control coast
ca. 1000 B.C.E.–500 C.E.	**600s C.E.**	**700s–1100s**	**1551–1711**	**1711–1835**

Students wearing T-shirts decorated with a portrait of revolutionary leader Colonel Mu'ammar Gadhafi celebrate the anniversary of the 1969 revolution.

from the throne. Under Gadhafi's leadership, the Revolutionary Command Council took power.

Gadhafi's aims were to create a socialist state where everyone had equal opportunities and a fair share of the country's wealth. He insisted that Libya control its own oil industry and receive more than half its profits. He invested enormous sums in modernizing houses, roads, hospitals, and schools. He also improved water supplies and invested in high-technology farming.

Gadhafi's international policies have been controversial. From 1973 to 1994 Libya fought a costly war against its neighbor Chad over Chad's northern Aozou Strip (see CHAD). Gadhafi has also proposed political unions with many Arab states and a united Arab campaign of hostility toward the Jewish state of Israel. He has quarreled fiercely with many Western governments, especially the United States, accusing it of wanting to take over the world. He has also supported groups attempting to disrupt or overthrow governments in many parts of the world.

The United States and Libya clashed openly in 1986, when the U.S. claimed the

Ottomans rule again	Italy invades Libya; Libyan resistance to occupation	Libya becomes colony of Italy	World War II; Great Britain and its allies fight Italians and Germans in Libya	Libya independent; Sanusi leader becomes king
1835–1911	**1911–1931**	**1934**	**1939–1945**	**1952**

right to sail its warships close to the Libyan coast. Libya launched fighter planes toward the U.S. fleet. In retaliation the United States bombed the Libyan mainland.

Two years later a bomb exploded on a U.S. passenger aircraft above the Scottish town of Lockerbie. Gadhafi allowed the two men accused of the bombing to seek refuge in Libya. As a result, the United Nations imposed economic sanctions on Libya. In 1999 Libya finally agreed that the two accused be allowed to stand trial at a special court in the Netherlands and the UN sanctions were lifted.

Living conditions for most Libyan people have improved enormously since Colonel Gadhafi came to power. Libya now ranks as the richest country in Africa, and much of its wealth has been used to

benefit ordinary people. However, there has been a high price to pay for this good fortune in terms of personal freedom and human rights. Anyone who repeatedly speaks out against Colonel Gadhafi and his policies is likely to end up in prison. International human rights organizations report that torture and ill-treatment are common in Libyan jails; some critics of the government have been executed. Libya has also been accused of sending hit squads to kill enemies of the government living abroad.

A Mix of Arab and Berber

Most Libyan people are of mixed ancestry, descended from the ancient Berber inhabitants of northern Africa and from the Muslims who arrived from the seventh century onward. They speak the Arabic language and follow the Islamic faith.

A small number of Berber people who have not intermarried with Arabs remain in Libya. They live mostly in the northwestern region and preserve their own language, customs, and traditions (see ALGERIA and MOROCCO).

In the southern deserts are groups of Tuareg (TWAHR-ehg) peoples (see ALGERIA, MALI, and NIGER). Traditionally nomads who make their living from herding

This man makes a living by weaving on a hand loom in his home in Tripoli, Libya's capital city. Like the vast majority of Libyans who live along the coast, he is of mixed Berber and Arab descent.

Oil discovered	Colonel Mu'ammar Gadhafi leads revolution	War with Chad over Aozou Strip	U.S. jets bomb Libya	United Nations sanctions begin	United Nations sanctions lifted
late 1950s	**1969**	**1973–1994**	**1986**	**1992**	**1999**

278

camels, the Tuareg are related to the Berbers and are used to living in the inhospitable desert. They speak Arabic and also their own language, known as Tifinagh.

Communities of black Africans, known as the Harratin (HAH-rah-teen), have lived at oases in the southern desert for hundreds of years. The Tebu (TAE-boo), who number less than three thousand, are another group of black Africans who also live in the far south. Their economy is based on herding, farming, and growing dates. Families are organized into clans along the father's line.

Libya is also home to many hundreds of thousands of foreign workers from more than a hundred countries. Many are technical experts employed in the oil industry. Many also work on major construction projects, in health care, and in education.

Nine out of ten people live in northern towns and villages close to the coast. Workers at oil and gas drilling sites, the inhabitants of scattered oasis towns, and Tuareg nomads are some of the few people that live in the desert.

Riches from Oil

The state now owns most of the oil and gas companies operating in Libya, and the government has used the oil profits to modernize the country and improve social welfare. As a result, Libyans' lives have changed very rapidly.

In the past most Libyans were poor farmers and camel herders. Today only one in six people works on the land. In the

In the desert, Tuareg nomad men veil their faces. Veils are a symbol of Tuareg identity; they also protect Tuareg men's hair and face from dust.

north farmers keep cows, goats, sheep, and chickens to produce meat and eggs. They also grow wheat, barley, olives, dates, citrus fruits, vegetables, and peanuts on irrigated, fertilized fields. In the south they raise dates and fruit and keep camels. Five out of six people have modern urban or industrial jobs. The main industrial products are textiles, cement, natural gas, and gasoline, which is refined from Libyan oil.

Libya is seriously short of water. To solve this problem, it has begun work on the largest engineering project in the world, a massive pipeline that will be 15 feet (4.5 meters) in diameter and will bring water from aquifers deep under the desert to Libya's biggest cities on the Mediterranean coast. The project already carries water to the cities of Benghazi (ben-GAH-zee) and Tripoli. There are plans to extend the pipeline along the coast.

Green trees and a shady doorway welcome visitors to the ancient walled city of Ghadamis, which is built at an oasis in Libya's inhospitable northwestern desert.

Keeping Tradition Alive

Islam is the official religion of Libya, and it is followed by about 97 percent of the population. Islam guides social customs, influences art and architecture, and shapes the country's laws. Muslim customs, such as the ban on alcohol and pork products and on public entertainments that might be judged indecent, are strictly enforced. There are no nightclubs or bars.

Both men and women are expected to be modestly dressed. In cities professional men often wear Western-style clothes, and industrial workers throughout the country wear T-shirts and jeans or overalls. Whenever they leave home, women in towns and cities cover their clothes with

Living in the Desert

It is almost impossible to survive in the desert without the right kind of shelter. At midday, temperatures can soar to 122°F (50°C), and there is very little natural shade. Over the generations the people of the Libyan desert oasis town of Ghadamis (guh-DAH-mes) have worked out ways of making their desert homes as cool and comfortable as they can. Thick walls of mud bricks keep out the heat and are whitewashed to reflect back the sun's rays, another way of trying to keep cool. Most houses are built around little covered courtyards, with open skylights in the center. Rooms have cooling features such as domed roofs, which allow more air to circulate, and wind chimneys, which create drafts as they draw air through floor-level holes up and out the chimney.

Within the town walls, walkways between blocks of houses are also roofed to keep out the heat and glare of the sun. Little skylights, set in the roof at intervals, provide just enough light for passersby to see where they are going. Entering Ghadamis feels almost like going underground.

long, voluminous robes, which they can pull over their heads and use to cover their faces when they are in the streets or in the company of unrelated men. Few women in the country wear veils. In northern country areas and in the desert, many people still wear long, loose clothes. Such clothes are cool and comfortable in the tremendous heat of the desert.

Concrete and Mud, Caves and Tents

Most Libyans now live in concrete, single-story houses or high-rise apartment buildings in cities and towns. In many northern villages comfortable new houses are often built next door to older family homes, which may then be used for storage or for keeping goats.

On the northwestern Nafusah Plateau, where many Berber families live, some walled villages still stand, perched on steep mountain slopes, with fortified communal storehouses for grain and olive oil. Houses are also built inside mountain caves. In the desert, nomad peoples live in tents or in oasis towns.

Revolutionary Ideas

The revolutionary government passed laws to give women greater rights in marriage and divorce, equal pay for equal work, support for working mothers, and the opportunity to serve in the police and armed forces. Better education, better health care, and the chance for women in towns to work outside the home have changed many women's lives. Today women make up about 20 percent of the workforce. They are employed as teachers, doctors, nurses, and office workers. Women living in the countryside have always worked in small family businesses and on farms.

Politically, Libyan society is unique. Since 1977 the country has been ruled by peoples' committees based on local communities or on traditional social groups such as desert tribes. In theory they are extremely democratic, with everyone having the chance to have their say and influence decision making. In practice, however, ordinary people do not often speak out against powerful leaders, regardless of their own personal views. All the peoples' committees are linked to the supreme governing body, the General Peoples' Congress. Officially, this body makes all political decisions. However, Colonel Gadhafi still has tremendous power.

Health and Education

Good housing, clean water, and enough money to buy food have all led to dramatically improved living standards for Libyan people since 1969. The government has also used oil money to pay for hospitals and clinics and for training doctors and nurses. Life expectancy is high compared to other countries in Africa, with men living to an average age of sixty-three and women to about sixty-eight.

A Libyan family enjoys a day out at one of the country's many beautiful, sandy beaches. Honoring Muslim tradition, the women remain modestly clothed, even in the water.

281

Schooling is free and compulsory for children between the ages of six and twelve, but most stay on until they are sixteen. Libya has a very high literacy rate: almost 90 percent of men fifteen and older can read and write and almost 70 percent of all women can do the same. After sixteen many students continue their education at colleges and universities in Libya and overseas. Libyan students abroad tend to specialize in subjects that will help their country develop further, especially medicine, engineering, and agriculture.

Everyday Foods and Desserts

Due to its fast-growing population, desert landscape, and lack of water, Libya has to import around three-quarters of its food supplies. Libya's basic foodstuff is grain, usually wheat. This is milled and cooked as flat bread or couscous and eaten with meat stew or with onions, peppers, tomatoes, and eggs. Italian-style pasta is often served but with a sauce containing chickpeas and flavored with northern African herbs and spices, such as chili,

Traditionally Libyan meals are eaten from a communal dish. Diners help themselves to a small portion with their hands. Men often eat apart from women and children.

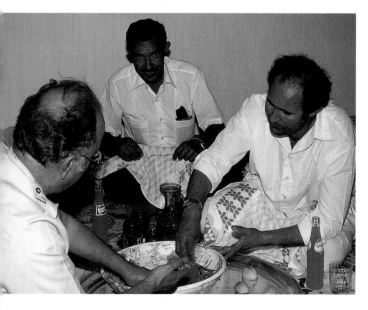

Zemeeta: Desert Cereal Sticks

Zemeeta (zuh-MEE-tah) is desert survival food: energy giving, easy to carry, and easy to store without cans or refrigeration. Zemeeta have a very strong flavor. People who are not used to very spicy foods might like to use about one-tenth of the spices listed here for starters. This quantity serves six people.

All quantities are approximate:
- *2 cups (500 grams) barley*
- *1 cup (250 grams) cumin seed*
- *1 cup (250 grams) coriander seed*
- *1 1/2 cups (375 grams) chopped, stoned dates*
- *6 tablespoons (100 grams) sugar*
- *a little olive oil and water to mix*

Boil the barley in water until soft, then drain. Stir drained barley and cumin and coriander seeds in a hot, dry frying pan or place them in a slightly warm oven, stirring occasionally, until lightly toasted. Leave to cool.

Pound or grind mixture until it is powdery. Mix chopped dates and sugar. Store in an airtight container.

To serve, pour a handful into a small bowl. Mix in water and olive oil, one tablespoonful (15 ml) at a time, until you have a solid lump. Don't make it too sticky. Roll small pieces of this between your fingers into sausage or stick shapes.

Zemeeta is dipped in more sugar and eaten with fresh dates and a glass of milk. Green tea follows, to end the meal.

coriander, and cinnamon. One specialty is
f'taat (fuh-TAHT), layers of wheat
pancakes, meat, and hard-boiled eggs with
a hot, spicy sauce. Middle Eastern-style
vegetables, such as eggplant, zucchini, and
tomatoes, stuffed with rice or couscous and
flavored with chopped onion and herbs,
are also popular.

Fresh fruit or dates grown in desert
oases satisfy the sweet tooth. Shops in
towns sell sweet, sticky pastries flavored
with honey and nuts in local style or based
on Italian recipes containing dried fruit.
Beverages include strong, black Turkish
coffee or Italian-style coffee with milk.
Sweet tea is also popular, as are carbonated
drinks and nonalcoholic beer.

Holidays and Festivals

Revolution Day (September 1) is the most
important holiday in Libya. It marks the
day in 1969 when Colonel Gadhafi came to

Inside the covered streets of the oasis town of Ghadamis, these men and boys have gathered for a friendly meeting and to make music on shawm (a kind of oboe) and drums.

power. Celebrations include army rallies,
marching bands, and dramatic displays by
dancers and desert horsemen, which are
watched by festive onlookers.

At public festivals—and at community
parties or family celebrations like
weddings—Libyan people enjoy listening
to music and joining in traditional dances.
Musical styles vary, from Angham al
Badya, played by nomads from the
Cyrenaica (sir-uh-NAE-uh-kuh) region, to
Maloof, music influenced by tunes from
Muslim Spain. Maloof is popular in
Tripoli. Some musicians are inspired by
music from Arabia. Others learn from
African performers in lands south of the
Sahara. There are also Libyan rock bands,
satirical singers, and popular radio folk-
music programs in which listeners are
invited to perform.

Glossary

AIDS: *a*cquired *i*mmuno*d*eficiency *s*yndrome, a normally fatal disease often passed on by sexual intercourse. It is caused by the virus HIV (*h*uman *i*mmunodeficiency *v*irus), which attacks the body's ability to resist disease and infection.

aquifers: large pools and streams of water trapped deep underground between layers of rock.

bauxite: a mineral from which aluminum is made.

bush: areas of forest or scrub remote from human settlements.

capitalist (policies): decisions based on an economic system in which land, factories, and other ways of producing goods are owned and controlled by individuals, not the government.

cardamom: a sweet spice often used in Asian cooking.

cassava: a plant with fleshy tuber roots, used as a food.

catchment: any hollow or tank used to catch rainwater.

cease-fire: a military order to stop fighting.

CFA franc: franc de la Communauté Financière Africaine (franc of the African Financial Community). This is a unit of currency shared by various African countries that were formerly French colonies.

cholera: a disease caused by drinking polluted water. It is marked by severe gastrointestinal symptoms and a very high temperature.

communism: a theory that suggests that all property belongs to the community and that work should be organized for the common good.

   communist: someone who believes in the theory of communism.

concession: a right that has been granted.

coup: a change of government brought about by force.

dysentery: a disease caused by bacteria or amoebas found in polluted water. It causes serious sickness and diarrhea.

expatriate: someone who lives in a country that is not his or her own; someone who withdraws allegiance to their own country.

foreign debt: money owed to foreign governments or companies.

guerrilla: a member of an irregular fighting force whose tactics include ambushes, surprise attacks, or sabotage rather than intense, close battles with the enemy.

herbalist: a healer who makes medicines from plants.

HIV-positive: infected with the virus (*h*uman *i*mmunodeficiency *v*irus) that causes the disease AIDS.

house arrest: an official order banning someone from leaving their home.

human rights abuses: human rights are conditions that many people believe are deserved by all human beings, such as freedom, equality, or justice. Abuses are acts that deny people such rights. Examples of abuses might include torture, censorship, or imprisonment without trial.

inflation: rising prices, with currency falling in value.

Koranic schools: classrooms attached to mosques (buildings where Muslim people pray). Boys go there to learn how to read Arabic and to study the faith of Islam.

liberals: people with moderate political opinions.

millet: a hardy cereal crop grown for food, drink, and fodder.

plantain: a fruit similar to the banana. It is a staple food in many tropical countries.

political refugees: people who leave their own country because they fear they may be punished for their political opinions.

protectorate: a territory that is given the protection of a more powerful state. In the colonial period in Africa the "protection" was often just a ploy by European countries to achieve political control of the territory.

republic: a country in which power rests with the people and their elected representatives. A president usually heads a republic.

sarong: a length of cloth, normally cotton, wrapped around the body. *Sarong* is originally a Southeast Asian word.

savanna: a grassland dotted with trees and drought-resistant undergrowth.

social welfare: services that aim to help people with problems such as poverty, unemployment, poor public health, and illiteracy.

sorghum: a grain crop commonly grown in hot countries.

subtropical: of, related to, or being the regions bordering the tropics, where the climate is warmer than in temperate regions.

temperate climate: having a moderate temperature year-round.

trade union (or labor union): an organization of workers formed to benefit workers by trying to raise wages and improve working conditions.

vote rigging: falsifying the results of an election, for example, by having people vote more than once for a candidate.

Further Reading

Internet Sites

Look under Countries A to Z in the Atlapedia Online Web Site at
     http://www.atlapedia.com/online/countries
Look under country listing in the CIA World Factbook Web Site at
     http://www.odci.gov/cia/publications/factbook
Look under country listing in the Library of Congress Country Studies Web Site at
     http://lcweb2.loc.gov/frd/cs/cshome.html

Guinea-Bissau

Nwanunobi, C. O. *Malinke.* New York: Rosen Group, 1996.

Ivory Coast

Krummer, Patricia K. *Cote d'Ivoire (Ivory Coast).* Danbury, CT: Children's Press, 1996.

Kenya

Ayodo, Awuor, and Atieno Odhiam. *Luo.* New York: Rosen Group, 1996.
Burch, Joann Johansen. *Kenya: Africa's Tamed Wilderness.* Minneapolis, MN: Dillon Press, 1996.
Hetfield, Jamie, and Johnson, Marianne. *The Maasai of East Africa.* New York: Powerkids
     Press, 1996.
Holtzman, Jon. *Samburu.* New York: Rosen Group, 1995.
Houston, Dick. *Safari Adventure.* New York: Cobblehill, 1991.
Ifemesia, Chieka. *Turkana.* New York: Rosen Group, 1995.
Kabira, Wanjiku Mukabi. *Agikuyu.* New York: Rosen Group, 1995.
Kagda, Falaq. *Kenya.* Milwaukee, WI: Gareth Stevens, 1997.
Pateman, Robert. *Kenya.* Tarrytown, NY: Benchmark Books, 1993.
Zeleza, Tiyambe. *Akamba.* New York: Rosen Group, 1995.
Zeleza, Tiyambe. *Maasai.* New York: Rosen Group, 1994.
Zeleza, Tiyambe. *Mijikenda.* New York: Rosen Group, 1995.

Lesotho

See web sites mentioned above

Liberia

Levy, Patricia. *Liberia.* Tarrytown, NY: Benchmark Books, 1998.
Stewart, Gail. *Liberia.* New York: Crestwood House, 1992.

Libya

Gottfried, Ted. *Libya: Desert Land in Conflict.* Brookfield, CT: Millbrook Press, 1994.
Lerner Publications. *Libya in Pictures.* Minneapolis, MN: Lerner Publishing Group, 1996.
Malcolm, Peter. *Libya.* Tarrytown, NY: Benchmark Books, 1996.

Index

Page numbers in *italic* indicate illustrations.

Page numbers in *italic* indicate illustrations.